SCHOLASTIC

GRAPHIC ORGANIZERS
for Teaching Poetry Writing

BETSY FRANCO

NEW YORK • TORONTO • LONDON • AUCKLAND • SYDNEY **Teaching** *Resources*
MEXICO CITY • NEW DELHI • HONG KONG • BUENOS AIRES

For Lottie

"Hey, Daddy Longlegs" by Betsy Franco was adapted from "Critter in My Bedroom"
copyright © 2006 by Betsy Franco from *Really Good Reader's Theater, Poems for Two or More Voices*.
Really Good Stuff: Monroe, CT, 2006. Used with permission.

Edited by Kathleen M. Hollenbeck
Cover design by Maria Lilja
Interior design by Sydney Wright
Cover and interior artwork by Mike Moran and Bari Weissman

ISBN-13: 978-0-439-53151-1
ISBN-10: 0-439-53151-9

Copyright © 2008 by Betsy Franco
Published by Scholastic Inc.
All rights reserved.
Printed in the U.S.A.

2 3 4 5 6 7 8 9 10   40   15 14 13 12 11 10 09

Contents

Poems and Lessons

Introduction

Traditionally, teachers introduce poetry forms in the upper elementary grades. But there's no need to wait! Using a simple, fun approach, *Graphic Organizers for Teaching Poetry Writing* will awaken the imaginations of young children and spark their desire and motivation to write.

In this resource, you'll find 20 different forms of poetry. Each original, sample poem is accompanied by a customized graphic organizer as well as detailed scaffolding dialogue to help students arrange and develop their thoughts. This combination of tool and technique will help you guide your young poets to create their best writing in each poetry form.

The poems and lessons in this collection also offer children the opportunity to practice and build skills in key elements of oral fluency, including intonation, phrasing, pace, and automaticity. (See page 9, for more.) Use the discussion suggestions to deepen comprehension and teach children to recognize the characteristics of different poetry forms, helping them make these forms their own when they write. The lessons are simple and ready-to-go, providing structure, guidance, and support as your young writers create.

Some of the poetry forms are traditional, such as haiku, limerick, acrostic, and concrete poems. Others are less well known or have been created for primary use, such as the memory poem, question poem, and action word poem. Graphic organizers bring all of these forms within reach.

It's always easier for children to create if they have a springboard to raise them to new heights. *Graphic Organizers for Teaching Poetry Writing* will serve that purpose for your students, helping them to organize thoughts and develop writing skills—and sharpening their reading comprehension and fluency to boot!

A Look at the Lessons

Each lesson includes:

◇ a reproducible poetry page featuring an original sample poem in a different poetry form. You may choose to distribute copies of the page to each student, copy the page onto a transparency for use with an overhead, or write the poem on chart paper.

◇ step-by-step instructions that provide scaffolding for sharing the poem with students and for guiding them to use the graphic organizer to write their own poems. Poetry tips, sprinkled throughout the book, offer additional teaching notes, suggestions, and inspiration. See Talk About the Poems, page 10, for more.

◇ a reproducible graphic organizer especially designed for each poetry form. In addition to giving each child a copy, you may want to copy the graphic organizer onto an overhead to use in your lesson. Enlarge the organizers when photocopying, if desired.

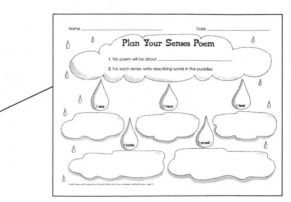

Guiding With Graphic Organizers

Primary teachers often struggle to engage students in writing. For young children, writing can be more of an imposition than art. Beyond generating ideas, children physically labor to form and spell words, let alone create meaning or beauty from them. They are asked to envision a whole, yet must overcome so many challenges in the process that they lose focus, motivation, and voice. What results is most often a weak, vague attempt at creative expression . . . and not much desire to do it again.

Graphic Organizers Collect Ideas

While the ideas are fresh in the mind, young writers jot them onto a graphic organizer. As they answer the questions and/or complete the organizer, their own thoughts and images—the meat of their writing—are preserved. The mechanics of grammar can come later; they won't block the train of thought now.

Graphic Organizers Offer Structure

They lead writers through a logical sequence, helping writers stay focused, organized, and motivated—moving from beginning to end. Sometimes, the organizer offers questions or prompts:

What memory will you tell about?

1. I remember when . . .

2. Here's how I felt at first . . .

3. Then I felt this way . . .

4. This is how I felt at the end . . .

Other times, the organizer directs:

- What will your first character say?
  Write those words in bubble 1.

- What will the other character say?
  Write those words in bubble 2.

If the writer follows such prompts step-by-step, the writer will have what he or she needs to create a finished product that makes sense and clearly expresses feelings, thoughts, or understandings.

"Graphic organizers are teaching tools that appeal to all types of students. They help visual learners *see* what you are trying to convey and provide a structure that helps children with limited attention spans stay focused." (Drapeau, 1998)

Scaffolding for Success

Scaffolding involves supporting and guiding a learner until the child can perform a desired skill on his or her own. Just as a parent holds the back of a bicycle and gradually lets go as the young rider achieves balance, a teacher who scaffolds shows students how to accomplish a skill—and then reduces the amount of instruction and modeling until the student has internalized the learning and is able to perform independently. By its very nature, scaffolding is teaching, with the intent of supporting all learners until they no longer need such guidance.

Scaffolding includes modeling specific strategies and ways of thinking, but it also involves carefully observing each learner and deciding which strategies will work best for that particular child. Some children will need repeated modeling and direction while others will grasp the concept right away.

Why Scaffold?

Regardless of varied abilities, the goal of scaffolding is the same for all: to bring each child from instruction to independence. Scaffolding engages students and creates motivated, successful learners. As they scaffold, teachers aren't simply modeling what they want children to do; they are guiding them step-by-step— giving young writers not only a vision, but also a roadmap. They are leading and supporting each writer's efforts toward mastery.

How Do I Scaffold?

At its simplest, scaffolding is three-part: the teacher determines what needs to be taught, chooses which strategies will help learners best grasp the concept, and breaks the teaching into manageable steps. As with any other successful teaching strategy, scaffolding practiced regularly and modified based on student performance can quickly become second-nature and an integral part of instruction.

> "If a writer does not understand the intention of instruction, the teacher must scaffold the student in ways that allow him to develop some degree of understanding. The level of teacher scaffolding is adjusted according to the needs of the young writer." (Dorn & Soffos, 2001)

How Do Graphic Organizers Relate to Scaffolding?

Studies suggest that to maximize the impact of graphic organizers on student learning, teachers need to state the purpose for using the organizer, model how to use it, and provide students with multiple opportunities for guided and independent practice and feedback. (National Center on Accessing the General Curriculum, 2002) Pairing graphic organizers with scaffolded instruction creates a win-win situation. Children get the tools they need for success . . . and the guidance on how to use those tools effectively.

Tips for Successful Scaffolding

Meet Learners Where They Are

Scaffolding is intended to teach, so the material presented must be at the student's instructional level. If the concept or skill is too difficult, the child may lose interest and the desire to achieve. To do this, first assess your students' individual needs. What are the student's current skills? What strategies will be most helpful in guiding him or her to create the poem? Each learner will approach the concept with his or her own learning style, experience, and skill level. It is the challenge of the effective teacher to identify these differences and find ways to engage and empower each writer. Does this mean creating a separate curriculum for each student? Not at all; rather, it means making slight adaptations on the spot; thinking in real time with intent to engage.

> "... scaffolding student learning might better be thought of as augmenting quality teaching rather than as a whole-sale change in teaching. In other words, if you live in a nice house where everything works well except for the television, which does not receive Channel 6, no one is asking you to buy a new house with a television that works— merely that you change the channel on the television to one that works." Rodgers & Rodgers, 2004)

Introduce Strategies

Different poems require different approaches. Sensory verse calls for meditating on texture, sound, taste, color, and scent. Concrete poems demand careful placement of words to form shapes, while rap poems must be recited again and again with an ear toward rhythm and beat. As you introduce each type of poem, make students aware of the strategies that bring forth the best features of each and you'll help generate depth, richness, and authenticity.

> "To know ways to help, we need to teach on our toes, expecting children to need coaching in ways that surprise us. How crucial it is to look honestly at what your children are actually doing and to believe your teaching can address issues you see."
> (Calkins & Parsons, 2003)

Revisit and Revamp

Some students will run with the ball; others will wait at length for the pass. Teachers who scaffold pass the ball repeatedly, sometimes modeling multiple times, other times walking the writer through the thought process:

Describe the way the grass feels under your bare feet.

- Does it tickle or scratch?
- Is it hot, cool, or warm?
- What does it feel like?
- Where were you the last time you stepped on wet grass?
- What do you remember about it?
- What words tell me what you remember?

Allow for Differences

While some students will create their own unique poems, filled with fresh ideas and agendas from the start, others will mimic whatever you've shown them. If you model a poem about snowflakes, you may expect at least three poems in class to be icy—and remarkably similar to yours! Embrace this imitation at first. For some students, it will take a while to feel comfortable writing poetry of their own; until then, they will follow your trail. (Hence, the success of cookbooks: many fine chefs only dare to sprinkle at will after years of adding precisely the amount of salt, pepper, and thyme called for in a well-loved recipe. They first need to gain their own sense of the art.)

Read Aloud

Poetry comes from the heart but is meant for the ears. No quality poem can come of silence; its words beg to be read aloud, tried out, replaced, repeated, moved, and selected again. Encourage your young writers to read their work aloud again and again, making sure each word makes sense where it is and says just what they want it to say. As they read their own writing aloud, children will improve reading fluency, learn the sound of their own writing voice, and appraise their work as they go.

"Reading fluency refers to the ability of readers to read quickly, effortlessly and efficiently with good, meaningful expression." (Rasinski, 2003) The length and natural rhythm of many poems lend themselves to fluency practice. Important elements of fluency include:

automaticity: the ability to recognize words automatically and read them accurately and smoothly

prosody: the ability to read a text orally using appropriate pitch, tone, and rhythm

rate: the pace at which one reads

intonation: the expressive emphasis given to particular words or phrases

Phrasing: understanding how to put words together in meaningful chunks and recognize natural phrase boundaries

> "It takes concentration to discuss a poem since a lot of meaning is packed into a few words. It's like a guessing game or puzzle that has no correct answer. Your students' responses will show you where they empathize with the poem." (Franco, 2005)

Talk About the Poems

Suggested questions for discussing the poems with your students follow. (Choose three or four questions for each poem.)

◇ Does anything stand out as unusual or different in the poem?

◇ What does the mood seem to be—angry, joyous, sad, silly?

◇ What is the poet's tone—serious, gentle, joking?

› How does the poem look on the page?

› What are your favorite words or phrases?

› Which words sound good together?

› What was surprising in the poem?

› Where there parts you didn't understand or didn't like? Where?

› Have you ever felt the way the poet does?

(Franco, 2005)

Poetry Writing Tips

› Although rhyme is a common aspect of children's poetry and makes it fun to read, it's deceptively complex to write. I recommend that students do not try to rhyme in their poems, except in the forms that require it such as limericks, blues, and rap poems.

› Remind children that the pictures on the organizers (clouds and raindrops, cans of paint, backpacks, acorns, and so on) are there simply to help them identify and organize their ideas—their poems can be on any topic of their choosing.

› Emphasize to children that the words, phrases, and sentences they write on the organizer don't have to be the same as the ones in their poems. The organizer is meant to help children develop ideas and structure for the poem. Children can and should feel free to make changes as they write.

◇ After children write their poems, try this extra challenge: Ask them to mix up the lines, putting them in different order. Discuss what difference this makes to the poem. Does it sound the same, better, or not as good? Does the meaning change at all? If so, in what ways?

Meeting the Standards for Language Arts

Mid-Continent Research for Education and Learning (McREL), a nationally recognized nonprofit organization, has compiled and evaluated national and state standards—and proposed what teachers should provide for their students to grow proficient in language arts, among other curriculum areas. The lessons and activities in this book support grades 2-4 students in meeting the following McRel standards:

◇ Uses the general skills and strategies of the writing process including the stylistic and rhetorical aspects of writing

⟩ Uses prewriting strategies to plan written work (discusses ideas with peers, uses graphic organizers, draws pictures to generate ideas, writes key thoughts and questions)

◇ Uses strategies to draft and revise written work (rereads; rearranges words to improve or clarify meaning; adds descriptive words and details; deletes extraneous information; incorporates suggestions from peers and teachers; sharpens the focus)

◇ Uses strategies to edit and publish written work (edits at a developmentally appropriate level; uses available, appropriate technology to compose and publish work; shares finished product)

◇ Writes in a variety of forms or genres including poetry

◇ Uses descriptive words to convey basic ideas and sensory details

◇ Uses grammatical and mechanical conventions in written compositions

◇ Uses nouns, verbs (for a variety of situations, action words), adjectives (descriptive words) adverbs (words that answer how, when, where, and why questions)

⟩ Uses conventions of spelling and punctuation in written compositions

◇ Uses the general skills and strategies of the reading process

◇ Reads aloud familiar poems with fluency and expression (rhythm, flow, meter, tempo, pitch, tone, intonation)

Source: Kendall, J.S. & Marzano, R. J. (2004). *Content knowledge: A compendium of standards and benchmarks for K–12 education.* Aurora, CO: Mid-continent Research for Education and Learning.

Ways to Extend the Poems

While the poems in this book were carefully written with the purpose of teaching young poets to write, they are also abundant in potential teaching angles. Lively and descriptive, the verse is linguistically rich, appealing in sound and imagery, and filled with opportunities to explore word use, phonics, and poetic characteristics such as onomatopoeia, rhythm and rhyme, simile and metaphor, and placement of words on the page. Try any of the following activities to enrich your students' experience of poetry.

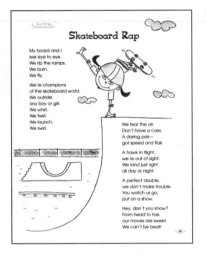

Connect With Phonics and Grammar

Use the poems to support specific phonics or word study skills your class is working on. Send pairs of students on a hunt through the poem "Ode to Pizza" (page 45), searching for blends and digraphs such as those found in _cheese_, _stick_, and _crunches_. The poem "Skateboard Rap" (page 49) is filled with _r_-controlled vowels. On a grammar note, "Soggy Field" (page 33) is chock-full of adjectives, and "Skateboard Rap" is almost entirely made up of action words! (Challenge students to underline the action words and write synonyms for them or draw pictures to illustrate any of the exciting images described in either poem.)

Explore Onomatopoeia

Some of the most entertaining, tongue-tickling poems are those that contain onomatopoeia—words that capture sound by name. The poem "Sssssounds of Summer" (page 81) is specifically intended to explore realistic sounds, but what about others that aren't tagged as sound poems? In "What to Do With a Stick on the Way to School" (page 17), the word _swish_ imitates the sound of a swaying leaf. Help your students find _swish_ and other examples of onomatopoeia in the poem—_clickity-click_, _tappity-tap_ and _rappity-rap-rap-rap_. Have them mark the words with highlighters. Encourage children to say the words aloud as if they are leaves swaying and sticks clicking and tapping. Then ask them to help you list other words that imitate sounds, such as _buzz_, _moo_, _meow_, _bang_, _plop_, _zip_, _hiss_, _achoo_, _ring_, _woof_, and the _whooooo_ of an owl or a whirling wind. Extend the activity by asking children to cut out two magazine pictures that show action. Ask them to hold up both pictures and make a sound that would go with only one. Partners should listen to the sound and identify the picture it describes.

Capture the Voice

Read the same poem aloud in different ways—with expression, in monotone, pausing for line breaks and punctuation, reading without pause, and so on. Ask children to tell you which way sounds best. Talk about the reasons why poets place words and use punctuation to lead readers through the poem and ensure it is read as intended. Haiku (page 25) and "I Remember" (page 73) provide excellent opportunities for this.

Use Descriptive Imagery

Develop descriptive imagery through riddles. Ask each child to think of a specific room in his or her home or another location, such as a grocery store or library, and write words or sentences describing what they see, smell, taste, touch, and/or hear there. Have students read the clues out loud so classmates can guess the location.

Write Letter Poems

Writing letters is an effective means of exploring thoughts and feelings as well as heightening sensory awareness. Before they begin work on a poem, have your students write about their topic in the form of a letter or as a journal entry. Once they have explored the topic in this way, they will be more familiar with their feelings on it and inclined to write more authentic, richer poems. For letter-writing (soon-to-be-poetry) prompts, choose topics that ask for personal rather than general responses, such as "What is your favorite room in your home? Why do you like it best?"

Experiment With Rhyme

Have students locate the rhyming pairs in one of the poems. Photocopy several poems with rhyming words, such as "What Am I? (page 41), "Why?" (page 65), and the limericks (page 77). Cut 3- by 5-inch index cards in half and give each student four of these. Students are to find two rhyming pairs and write all four words on the index cards—one word per card. When finished, have children shuffle their cards with another player's cards and turn them facedown to play the matching game Concentration. Mix their cards with several classmates' and use the new deck to play a rhyming version of "Go Fish."

Incorporate Sounds

After reading the riddle poem "What Am I?" (page 41), have children write their own riddles for animals or objects, using sounds as clues. For example, they might mention the roar of a lion, the drumming of raindrops, or the click of a dog's nails on a hard floor.

Use Visualization

Help children develop the skill of descriptive imagery with this brief exercise. Have children sit in a circle on the rug or floor. Invite them to close their eyes and sit still for a moment while you speak softly and slowly. Say "Keep your eyes closed, and picture yourself in a place you really like. Stand there for a moment, and notice what is around you. What are you seeing, behind your closed eyes?" Ask children to keep their eyes closed. Say one child's name at a time, and have the child say and complete the sentence, "Just behind my eyelids, I see. . ."

Observe Details

Bring in several handheld mirrors and give one to each small group. Have students take turns studying their faces in the mirror and writing words that describe what they see: brown freckles, smooth skin, missing teeth, and so on. Use this to create either a list poem or a "two-words-on-a-line" poem such as those on pages 17 and 33.

Explore Rhythm

Using the rap poem (page 49) as an example, help students create their own rhythmic poetry, set to the sound of fingers tapping on a desk or upturned paper cup.

Examine Word Choice

Copy a poem onto chart paper, but leave out several adjectives. Ask children to think of words they might use to enhance the poem. Poems well suited to this are "Soggy Field" (page 33), "Ode to Pizza" (page 45), and the diamond poems (page 69).

Consider Point of View

Point out the varied perspectives used in poems throughout the book: first-person "Skateboard Rap" (page 49), second-person "Ode to Pizza" (page 45), third-person diamond poems (page 69) and limericks (page 77). Throughout the year, as you introduce poems from this book and from anthologies, have students identify the speaker of the poem.

Study Metaphor in Literature

Read aloud picture books rich in simile and metaphor, such as Jane Yolen's *Owl Moon* (Philomel, 1987) and Audrey Wood's *Quick as a Cricket* (Child's Play International, 1990). Point out several phrases that compare items, such as *"The trees stood still as giant statues,"* and *"They sang out, trains and dogs, for a real long time."* (Yolen, 1987) Help children understand the reasons why the author chose to compare these specific items—to paint a picture that helps the reader see what the author envisions. Then help them locate other examples in the story. As a group, create your own comparative prose to add to the story.

Keep a Poetry Journal

Help children make miniature poetry journals to hold their ideas for future poems. To make the booklets, cut manuscript paper into 3- by 5-inch pieces. Have each student count out 20 sheets of the paper and stack them to make a small booklet. Hold the child's booklet horizontally and staple it along the left edge to hold the pages together. Then cover the booklet with wallpaper and staple again. Place a small strip of duct tape over the staples to cover the sharp ends. Let each child use permanent marker to write his or her name on the book. Store them in student desks or in a small shoe box for easy access.

Resources

Atwell, N. (2002). *Lessons That Change Writers*. Portsmouth, NH: Heinemann.

Calkins, L. & Parsons, S. (2003). *Poetry: Powerful Thoughts in Tiny Packages*. Portsmouth, NH: Heinemann.

Calkins, L. (1994). *The Art of Teaching Writing*. Portsmouth, NH: Heinemann.

Dorn, L. J. & Soffos, C. (2001). *Scaffolding Young Writers: A Writers' Workshop Approach*. Portland, ME: Stenhouse Publishers.

Drapeau, P. (1999). *Great Teaching With Graphic Organizers*. New York: Scholastic.

Franco, B. (2005). *Conversations With a Poet: Inviting Poetry Into K–12 Classrooms*. Katonah, NY: Richard C. Owens Publishers.

Hall, T. & Strangman, N. (2002). *Graphic Organizers*. Wakefield, MA: National Center on Accessing the General Curriculum.

Rasinski, T. V. (2003). *The Fluent Reader*. New York: Scholastic.

Rodgers, A. & Rodgers, E. M., (2004). *Scaffolding Literacy Instruction: Strategies for K-4 Classrooms*. Portsmouth, NH: Heinemann.

Urquhart, V. & McIver, M. (2005). *Teaching Writing in the Content Areas*. Alexandria, VA: Association for Supervision and Curriculum Development.

What to Do With a Stick on the Way to School

Let it *clickity-click* along the sidewalk in front of you.

Swish the leaves hanging down from a tree branch.

Conduct an invisible orchestra.

Lean on it if you get tired.

Stir a puddle and see what's in there.

Rescue a worm that you find in the puddle.

Poke around in the soggy ground.

And best of all,

tappity-tap, rappity-rap-rap-rap

it on the long school fence made of steel,

before you have to leave it outside the classroom

because the teacher says no sticks in class.

Writing a List Poem

Activate Prior Knowledge

Ask children why people use *lists*. Assist them in recognizing that people make lists to help themselves

◇ remember things they want to buy or do;

◇ organize tasks;

◇ keep track, as with attendance or lunch count.

Invite children to name various kinds of lists that people keep, such as grocery lists, guest lists, and wish lists.

Share the Poem

1. Distribute copies of the poem (page 17), write it on chart paper, or copy it onto an overhead transparency.

2. Explain that today's poem is a *list poem*—a poem that is also a list. Invite children to read the title aloud with you. Then ask them to predict what the list poem might tell them, based on its title.

3. Read the poem aloud twice— once to children and the second time, as they read along.

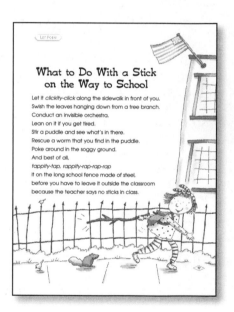

4. Invite children to point out the various uses that the poem suggests for a stick. Highlight these uses by circling them in colored marker.

Scaffold Using the Graphic Organizer

1. Tell children that the class will plan and write a list poem. As a class, brainstorm topics that would generate many ideas for a list, such as "What I Do When It Snows," "What I Do to Get Ready for School in the Morning," or "My Favorite Foods." Choose one topic that you will use to demonstrate how to organize and write a list poem.

2. Photocopy and distribute the graphic organizer (page 20). If possible, copy the organizer onto an overhead transparency or enlarge it so that you can model how to use it.

3. Write the topic on the top leaf. This will also be the title.

4. Ask children to list four ideas that go with the topic. Write these on the remaining four leaves.

5. When you have four ideas, ask the class to read over the list and then order the ideas the way they want them to appear in the poem. Put a number next to each idea to indicate which will come first, second, third, and so on.

6. On chart paper, rewrite the poem by putting the ideas in the order you've all determined is best. Read the list poem out loud, and then ask:

◇ Does our poem make sense?

⟩ Do we need to add or take out words to make our poem easier to read?

◇ Did we say everything we wanted to say in our poem?

On the same day or during another session, reread the poem and remind children of the steps they took to write it. Then give them a fresh copy of the graphic organizer and help them create their own poems—based on their own topics and ideas. Use the graphic organizers for rough drafts. When you feel children are ready, have them copy their poems onto lined paper without numbering them.

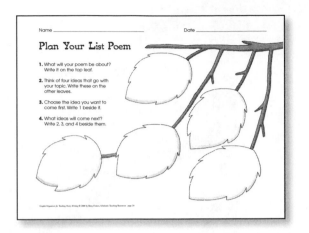

POETRY TIP

While helping children put the ideas in order, point out that many poets find something fun or interesting to grab a reader's interest at the start of the poem and leave something surprising, fun, or unusual for the end.

Plan Your List Poem

 1. What will your poem be about? Write it on the top leaf.

2. Think of four ideas that go with your topic. Write these on the other leaves.

3. Choose the idea you want to come first. Write 1 beside it.

 4. What ideas will come next? Write 2, 3, and 4 beside them.

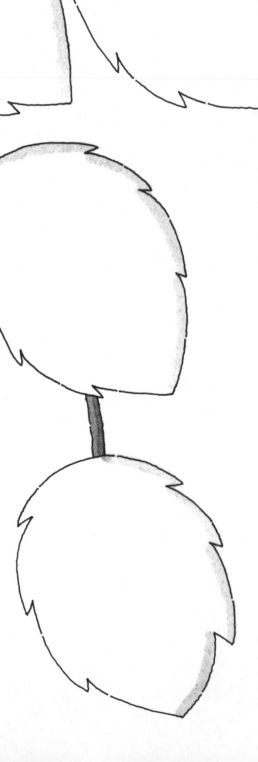

Thoughts of a Backpack

You stuff me
with books
    and lunch
      and a ball.
It's kind of hard to hold it all.

And then you forget
to empty me out.
That's when I wish
that I could shout!

'Cause I'm full
   of goo
     and lunch and junk
      and rot and mold,
all sorts of gunk.

But wait a minute . . . I'm not done.
Riding you piggyback really is fun.
I jounce
and bounce
as you run along
and my trinkets jangle
and clank
a song!

Writing a Personification Poem

Activate Prior Knowledge

1. Ask children to think of things dogs do, such as bark, chew bones, wag their tails, and run. Then show them a backpack and ask them to name things a backpack might do. Observe with children that backpacks don't *do* anything; they are not living and cannot move, think, or speak.

2. Explain that when a writer treats an object like a person, we call that *personification*. In a poem with personification, something that isn't a person seems to come alive. It may think, have feelings, and even speak.

Share the Poem

1. Distribute copies of the poem (page 21), write it on chart paper, or copy it onto an overhead transparency.

2. Explain that today's poem uses personification. Help children read the title out loud. Say: "Pretend that a backpack really could think. What kinds of thoughts might it have when it is empty or full?" Allow time for children to predict what the poem might tell them.

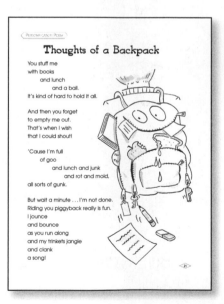

Personification Poem

Thoughts of a Backpack

You stuff me
with books
        and lunch
              and a ball.
It's kind of hard to hold it all.

And then you forget
to empty me out.
That's when I wish
that I could shout!

'Cause I'm full
    of goo
          and lunch and junk
              and rot and mold,
all sorts of gunk.

But wait a minute . . . I'm not done.
Riding you piggyback really is fun.
I jounce
and bounce
as you run along
and my trinkets jangle
and clank
a song!

3. Read the poem aloud once, and then invite children to read it with you. Ask: "Who's talking? Does this object usually talk? Why not?"

4. Invite children to discuss the backpack's mood at the beginning and end of the poem. What is it complaining about? What does it enjoy? Then ask, "If you were a backpack, might you feel the same way? Why? What are some things you might say to your owner?"

Scaffold Using the Graphic Organizer

1. Tell children that the class will plan and write a personification poem. Together, brainstorm a list of items that don't speak, such as an object (perhaps a chair or pencil), a force of nature (maybe the wind or a volcano), or an animal (such as a rabbit or bear). Choose one you will use to demonstrate how to plan and write a personification poem.

2. Photocopy and distribute the graphic organizer (page 24). If possible, copy the organizer onto an overhead transparency or enlarge it so that you can model how to use it.

3. At the top of the organizer, find the words "I am a _____." On the line, write the name of the object, force of nature, or animal the class has chosen, while students write the same name on their organizers.

4. Ask the following questions and write children's answers on the backpack pockets while they write the same answers on their own papers. (The questions below correlate with the prompts on the organizer.)

◌ Imagine what it would be like to be _____. How do you spend your time? (Write this beside: "This is what I do.")

◌ What makes you sad?

◌ What makes you happy?

> In what way might you like to change your life?

◌ What would you say to the person who owns or takes care of you?

5. Help children develop a poem based on the thoughts and ideas on the organizer. Together, create the poem on a sheet of chart paper or on the overhead.

6. On the same day or during another session, revisit the poem and remind children of the steps they took to write it. Then give them a fresh copy of the organizer. Following the same techniques used above, help children use the organizer to plan their own personifications poems. When you feel children are ready, have them write their poems on a separate sheet of paper.

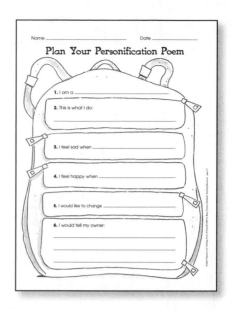

POETRY TIP

Point out that the backpack in the personification poem uses the word "I" because it is talking about itself. For example, it says, "That's when I wish that I could shout!" Encourage children to use this first-person voice in their personification poems.

Name _____   Date _____

Plan Your Personification Poem

1. I am a _____.

2. This is what I do:

_____

3. I feel sad when _____.

4. I feel happy when _____.

5. I would like to change _____.

6. I would tell my owner:

_____

_____

_____

Haiku

Meow at the door.
Kitty comes in from the rain.
Wet fur needs licking.

The flowers are gone
on my new marigold plants—
The snails are smiling.

Ants feeling cozy
on the dry kitchen counter.
Don't eat our dessert!

Writing Haiku

Activate Prior Knowledge

Ask children what comes to mind when they hear the word *nature*. Help them understand that plants, animals, and living things found outdoors are all part of what we call nature. Invite them to name some of these things, such as grass, leaves, ladybugs, caterpillars, and tree branches.

Share the Poem

1. Distribute copies of the Haiku (page 25), write them on chart paper, or copy onto an overhead transparency.

2. Tell children that today they will read and write poems about nature. These poems are called *Haiku*. Point out that there are three poems on the page. Each one is called Haiku. Explain that Haiku is a short poem that is written in just three lines. The middle line is the longest.

3. Read the Haiku aloud and then have children read along with you as they are able. Tell them that Haiku is written about small things in nature that are special, and that Haiku often gives a hint about what season it is.

4. Talk about what is happening in each Haiku: the cat coming in with wet fur, the snails eating the marigolds, the ants nearing the dessert on the kitchen counter. These are not big events, but they are interesting, they happen in nature, and (in some regions) they happen at specific times of the year.

5. Ask children to identify the season they believe each Haiku talks about and tell what clues they found in the poem that connect with that season.

6. Discuss how the three lines of each poem go together. For example, in the first Haiku: a kitty meows, a kitty comes inside, and a kitty licks its wet fur.

7. Next, point out the length of the lines. Explain that Haiku often has five syllables (beats or claps) in the first and last lines. The middle line often has seven. Help children clap out the syllables in all three poems.

POETRY TIP

Must-haves for Haiku include conciseness and observation—describing as vividly as possible *in as few words* as possible—based on authentic observation and use of the senses.

Scaffold Using the Graphic Organizer

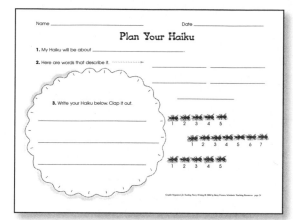

1. Tell children that the class will plan and write Haiku together. Brainstorm a list of possible subjects in nature, such as bugs, raindrops, or snowflakes. Choose one you will use to demonstrate how to plan and write Haiku. If you have time, it would be helpful to show children a real object or photograph of something from nature. A stick, a leaf, a butterfly . . . any of these will provide rich background material for Haiku when observed closely.

2. Photocopy and distribute the graphic organizer (page 28). If possible, copy the organizer onto an overhead transparency or enlarge it so that you can model how to use it.

3. Fill in the topic of the Haiku. With children's help, write words that describe the topic on the lines provided.

4. Explain that Haiku uses three lines but has no title, so, in step 3, the first words you write will be the first line of the poem. Have children use the descriptive words they brainstormed to help you write something about the topic on the first line. (Keep the line brief and don't interrupt your young writers' creative flow by counting syllables yet.)

5. Ask children to think of a second line that goes with the first but gives more information.

6. Do the same for the third line, encouraging children to wrap up the poem in some way. Tell them that sometimes the last line can be a bit of a surprise.

7. Help children read the finished poem and clap out its syllables, using the ant pictures as a guide. Make adjustments as needed to achieve the 5-7-5 syllable pattern. (See Poetry Tips, right.)

8. On the same day or during another session, revisit the Haiku and remind children of the steps they took to write it. Then give them a fresh copy of the organizer. Following the same techniques used above, help children use the organizer to plan their own Haiku. When you feel children are ready, have them copy their Haiku onto a separate sheet of paper.

POETRY TIPS

* With younger students, you may want to relax the syllable count. (Not all Haiku follow the 5-7-5 syllable pattern.) Have children add or cross out "ants" depending on the number of syllables they use in each line.

* If possible, provide opportunities for children to gather sensory details about Haiku subjects, by exploring outdoors or browsing through nature magazines such as The National Wildlife Federation's *Your Big Backyard* and *National Geographic Kids*. The more observation accrued, the more authentic and descriptive the Haiku.

Name _____

Date _____

Plan Your Haiku

1. My Haiku will be about _____

2. Here are words that describe it. ·············▸

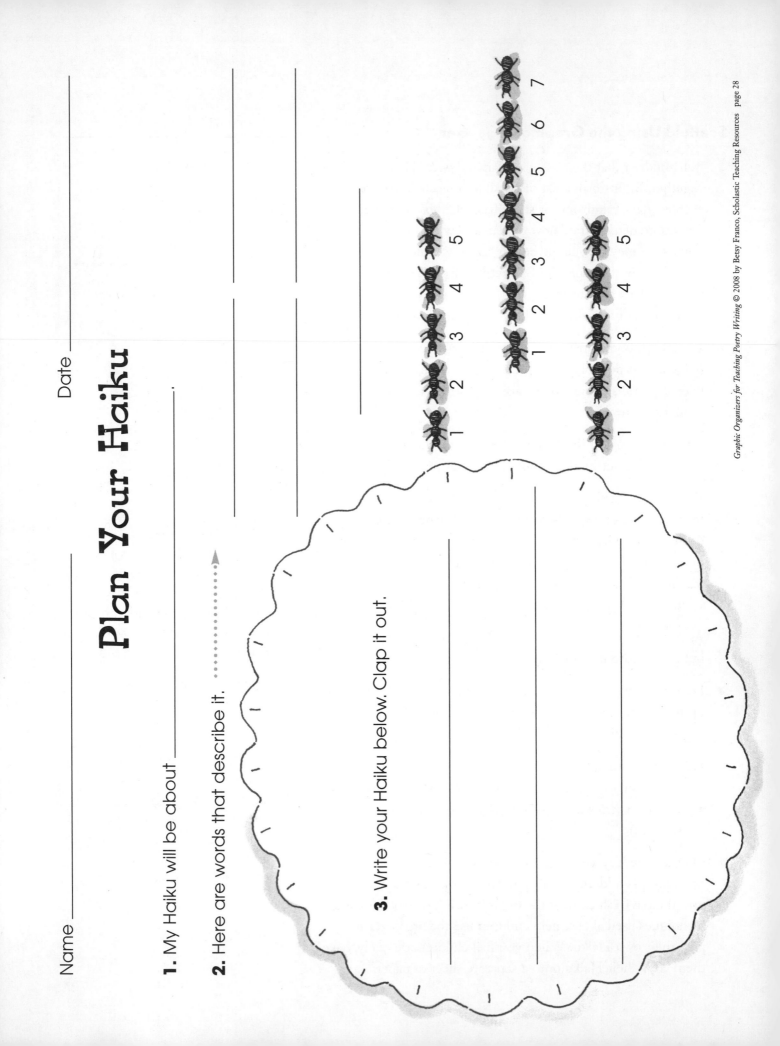

3. Write your Haiku below. Clap it out.

Brother Blues

My brother started it
He called me names.
My brother started it.
He called me names.
I got the blame.
I got the blame.

Sent to my room
to think it through.
Sent to my room
to think it through.
No video games.
No video games.

I've got the blues.
Wouldn't you?
I've got the blues.
Wouldn't you?

Writing a Blues Poem

Activate Prior Knowledge

Talk about a blues poem. Ask: "If you have the blues, what mood are you in?" Explain that people who "have the blues" are not blue in color; they are feeling sad. Sometimes people use the expression "I've got the blues" to let others know they are unhappy.

Share the Poem

1. Distribute copies of the poem (page 29), write it on chart paper, or copy it onto an overhead transparency.

2. Tell children that today they will read a poem about someone who has the blues. Read the poem aloud once and then invite children to read along with you. As you read, use your voice to emphasize the poem's rhythmic, repetitive beat.

3. Talk about the poem. Ask: "What is the child upset about? Have you ever gotten in trouble for something your brother or sister started? How did you feel?" Invite several volunteers to share their experiences with this.

4. Turn children's attention back to the poem. Ask them to find the repetition in the poem—the parts they hear more than once. Invite them to tell why the poet might have repeated those lines (*to emphasize the speaker's mood and how the child felt about what happened*).

Scaffold Using the Graphic Organizer

1. Explain to children that they will be writing a blues poem together. As a class, brainstorm a list of events or subjects that might bother a child, prompting him or her to complain, or feel angry or sad in some way. Examples include being left out of a group, treated unkindly by a friend, unfairly accused of something, or not being allowed to buy a coveted toy.

2. Choose one complaint that you will use to demonstrate how to plan and write a blues poem.

3. Photocopy and distribute the graphic organizer (page 32). If possible, copy the organizer onto an overhead transparency or enlarge it so that you can model how to use it.

4. At the top of the organizer, have students tell what the poem will be about.

5. Invite them to help you introduce the problem briefly, in the first two lines of the poem. Then have them repeat those lines, mimicking the style found in "Brother Blues."

6. Next, add another detail to the poem to develop the story. Repeat the line.

7. Continue in this way until you have written a brief blues poem. As you work together, remind children that the poem is meant to convey emotion and tell a story. (Tell children that rhyming is not necessary.)

8. On the same day or during another session, revisit your blues poem and remind children of the steps they took to write it. Then give them a fresh copy of the organizer. Following the same techniques used above (and described on the organizer), help children use the organizer to plan their own blues poems. When you feel children are ready, have them write their poems on a separate sheet of paper, without numbering the lines.

Name _____ Date _____

Plan Your Blues Poem

My blues poem is going to tell about when _____

1. Write the first two lines of your poem on steps 1 and 2.
2. Write the same two lines again on steps 3 and 4.
3. Write two new lines on steps 5 and 6.
4. Repeat the same two lines again on steps 7 and 8.
5. Repeat the process for the next four steps. Write two new lines and then repeat them. (The last two lines have been written for you.)

1.
2.
3.
4.
5.
6.
7.
8.
9.
10.
11.
12.
I've got the blues. Wouldn't you?
I've got the blues. Wouldn't you?

Plan Your Blues Poem

My blues poem is going to tell about when _____

_____.

1. Write the first two lines of your poem on steps 1 and 2.

2. Write the same two lines again on steps 3 and 4.

3. Write two new lines on steps 5 and 6.

4. Repeat the same two lines again on steps 7 and 8.

5. Repeat the process for the next four steps. Write two new lines and then repeat them. (The last two lines have been written for you.)

1.

2.

3.

4.

5.

6.

7.

8.

9.

10.

11.

12.

I've got the blues. Wouldn't you?

I've got the blues. Wouldn't you?

Soggy Field

Soggy field
Pounding feet
Panting breath
Spinning ball
Quick pass
Strong kick
Diving goalie
Screaming crowd
Winning goal!
High fives!

Writing a "Two-Words-on-a-Line" Poem

Activate Prior Knowledge

Write two describing words on the board, such as *enormous* and *warm*. Invite children to name an animal or object that each word might describe, such as *enormous dinosaur* and *warm blanket*. On chart paper or an overhead transparency, write each word pair on a separate line. Point out that two words together make a pair of words. Ask: "How many pairs of words did we make?" Explain that the first word in each of these pairs is a *describing* word. The second is a *naming* word. Invite children to list additional word pairs that include a descriptive word and a naming word. Examples might include: *furry puppy, scratchy sweater, leaky faucet,* and *spicy pizza*. Help children understand that two words together may not seem like much, but each pair of words can create a clear picture in someone's mind.

Share the Poem

1. Distribute copies of the poem (page 33), write it on chart paper, or copy it onto an overhead transparency.

2. Ask children what they notice about this poem. *(It is long and thin. There are only two words on each line.)*

3. Inform children that this kind of poem is a "two-words-on-a-line" poem. Invite them to tell why they think the poem has that name. Explain that in this poem, each line has only two words.

4. Read the poem aloud once. Then have children read along with you. Ask them to find a pattern in each line: *describing word, naming word.*

5. Invite children to point out their favorite pairs of words in the poem. Explain that these word pairs work together to tell a story. Ask: "What story is the poem telling us?"

Scaffold Using the Graphic Organizer

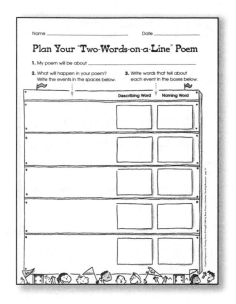

1. Tell children that today, they will be writing their own poem that is made up of word pairs and that first, you'll write one as a class.

2. Photocopy and distribute the graphic organizer (page 36). If possible, copy the organizer onto an overhead transparency or enlarge it so that you can model how to use it.

3. Choose a subject that lets you tell a story, such as a thunderstorm, a fire drill, or a bee sting at a picnic. Write the topic of the poem at the top of the organizer.

4. List five events that will happen in the poem to tell a story. Write these as sentences in the left column of the scoreboard.

5. With children's help, number each event to put the story in order.

6. Brainstorm a describing word and a naming word that will narrate each event (for example, the poet uses "spinning ball" to illustrate the event "The ball is rolling quickly down the field."). Write the words in the pair of score boxes next to each sentence.

7. On a blank overhead transparency or on a sheet of chart paper, create the poem by writing each pair of words where it will best tell its part of the story.

8. On the same day or during another session, revisit your "two-words-on-a-line" poem and remind children of the steps they took to write it. Then give them a fresh copy of the organizer. Following the same techniques used above, help children use the organizer to plan their own poems. When you feel children are ready, have them copy their poems onto a separate sheet of paper.

Name _____   Date _____

Plan Your "Two-Words-on-a-Line" Poem

1. My poem will be about _____

2. What will happen in your poem?
Write the events in the spaces below.

3. Write words that tell about
each event in the boxes below.

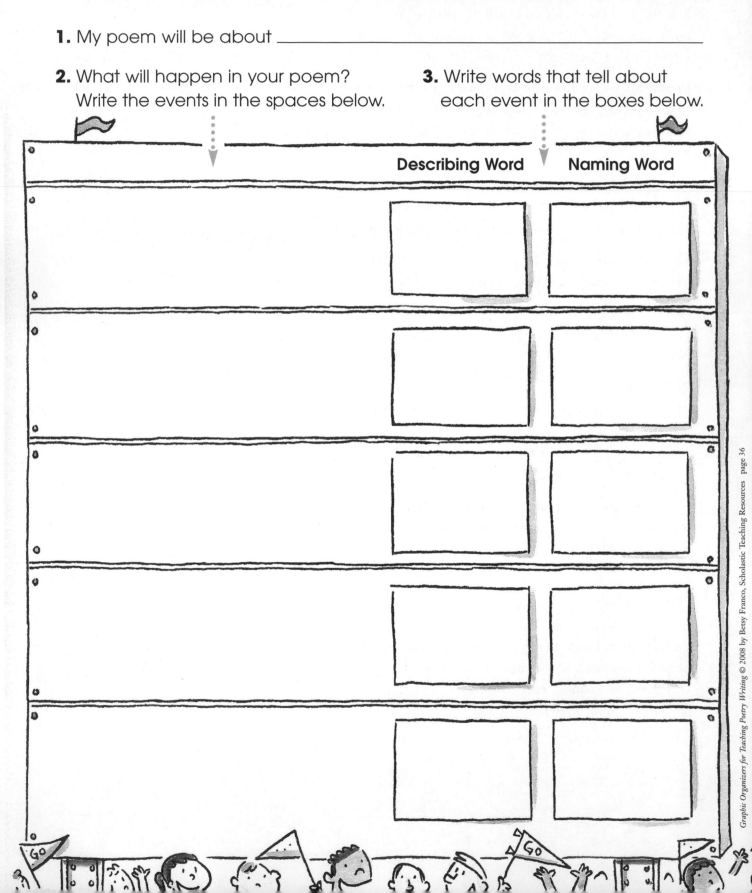

Describing Word   Naming Word

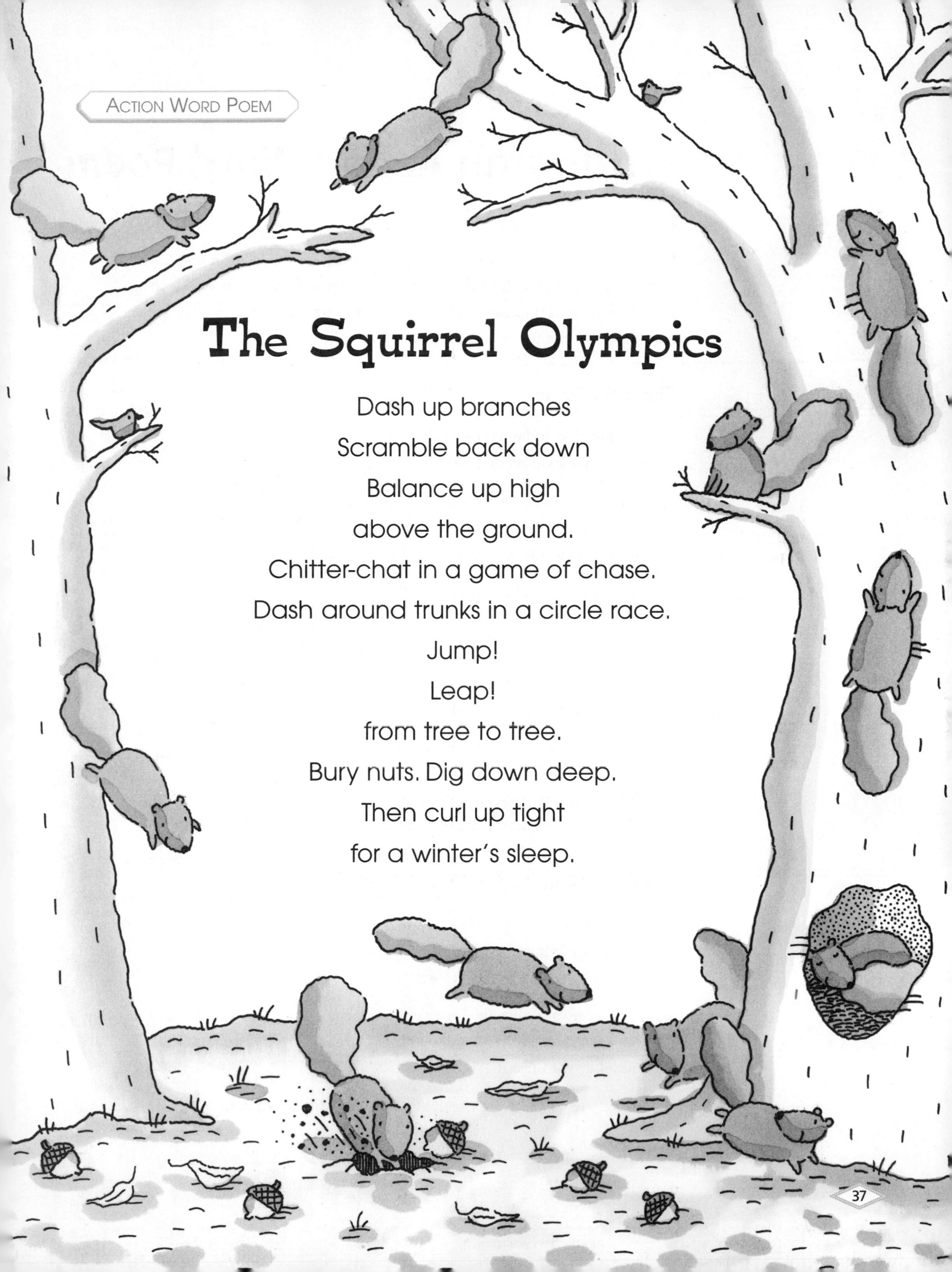

The Squirrel Olympics

Dash up branches

Scramble back down

Balance up high

above the ground.

Chitter-chat in a game of chase.

Dash around trunks in a circle race.

Jump!

Leap!

from tree to tree.

Bury nuts. Dig down deep.

Then curl up tight

for a winter's sleep.

Writing an Action Word Poem

Activate Prior Knowledge

Write several simple words on the chalkboard, such as *glass*, *jump*, *leap*, and *spoon*. Ask children to find the words that show action. Invite children to give their own examples of action words, and write these as well. Explain that action words tell what is happening.

Share the Poem

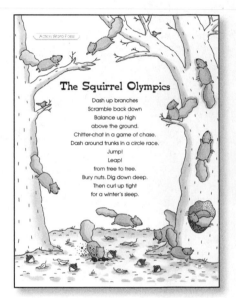

1. Explain that today you will share a poem that has lots of action words.

2. Distribute copies of the poem (page 37), write it on chart paper, or copy it onto an overhead transparency.

3. Read the poem aloud once and then invite children to read along with you.

4. Ask children to find the action words in the poem. Use a marker to highlight or underline the action words.

5. Discuss the idea that, in this poem, action words help tell a story. Help children realize that the action words tell how the squirrels spend their days.

Scaffold Using the Graphic Organizer

1. Tell children that the class will plan and write an action poem. Together, choose an animal, person, or object that brings to mind lots of action words, such as a kite, a kitten, or a dancer.

2. Photocopy and distribute the graphic organizer (page 40). If possible, copy the organizer onto an overhead transparency or enlarge it so that you can model how to use it.

3. Write the topic of the poem at the top of the organizer.

4. Help students generate six action words that come to mind when thinking about the topic. (For example, for kites, they might say *dip*, *soar*, *fly*, *race*, *rise*, and *dive*.) Write each word on one of the acorns on the organizer.

5. On chart paper, begin to build the poem by writing a short phrase or sentence using each action word (for example, *racing with the wind*).

6. In what order do children want to use the action phrases and sentences in their poem? Write a number beside each one. Then copy them, in order, on a fresh sheet of paper.

7. On the same day or during another session, give children a fresh copy of the organizer. Following the same techniques used above, help children plan their own action word poems. When they have finished writing the action words on the organizer, give each child a sheet of paper. Have children write a phrase or short sentence for each action word, then number the sentences in the order they want them to appear in their poem. When you feel children are ready, have them write their poems on a fresh sheet of paper.

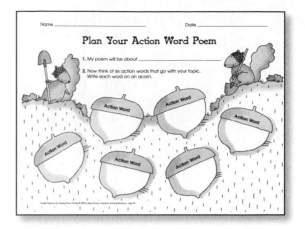

POETRY TIPS

* After children write their action word poems, try this extra challenge. Ask them to mix up the lines, putting them in a different order. Discuss what difference this makes to the poem. Does it sound the same, better, or not as good? Does the meaning change at all? In what ways?

* Stress that, like many poems, the words in an action word poem do not have to rhyme.

Name _____

Date _____

Plan Your Action Word Poem

1. My poem will be about _____

2. Now think of six action words that go with your topic. Write each word on an acorn.

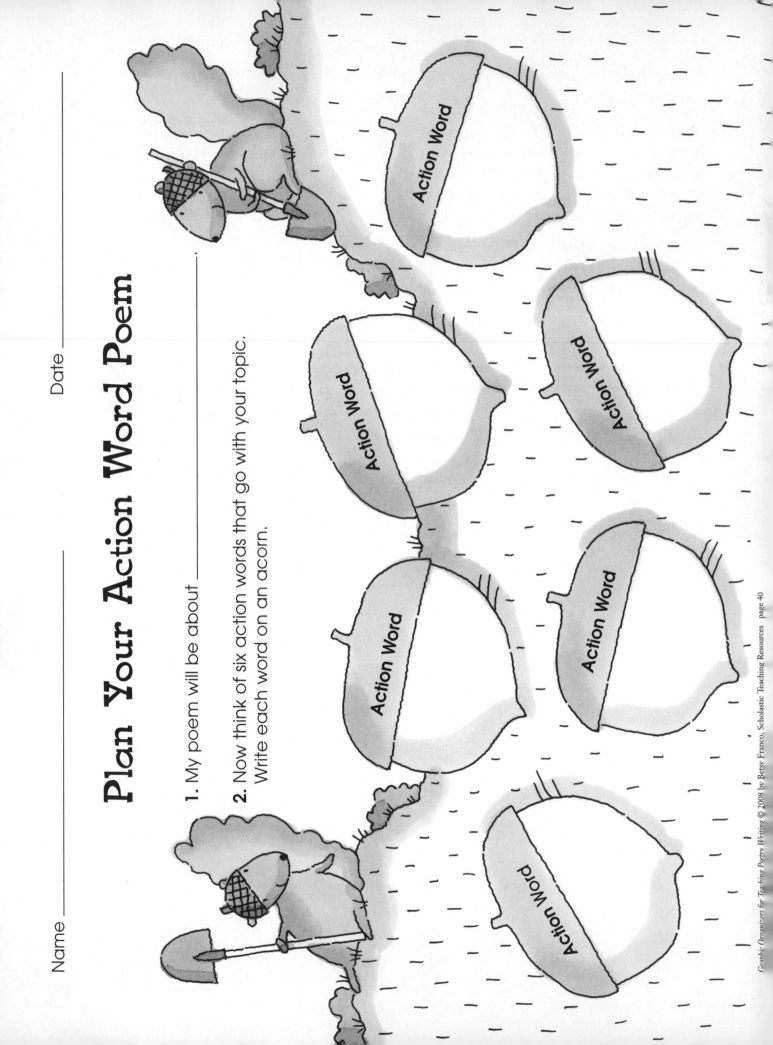

Action Word

Action Word

Action Word

Action Word

Action Word

Action Word

What Am I?

People use this on a train,
in a bus, or when
boarding a plane,

in a car,
on any street,
walking, running,
sitting in a seat.

Wherever you go,
you're sure to hear
someone talking
with this on an ear.

But if it rings in a movie show
everyone turns
and their stares say,
"NOOOO!
TURN IT OFF!
DON'T SAY, 'HELLO'!"

Writing a Riddle Poem

Activate Prior Knowledge

Talk with students about riddles. Ask: "What is a riddle?" Help them understand that a riddle gives clues for a person to solve. To demonstrate, you may want to share a riddle students might know, such as "What's black and white and read all over?" (*a newspaper*)

Share the Poem

1. Explain that today you will share a *riddle poem*.

2. Distribute copies of the poem (page 41), write it on chart paper, or copy it onto an overhead transparency.

3. Read the riddle poem aloud while students listen or read along with you.

4. Have children guess the answer to the riddle. (*a cell phone*)

5. Ask them to identify the hints within the riddle that helped them figure out the answer. Underline the clues with a highlighting marker.

Scaffold Using the Graphic Organizer

1. Tell children that they will be writing their own riddles. First, you will write one together.

2. Photocopy and distribute the graphic organizer (page 44). If possible, copy the organizer onto an overhead transparency or enlarge it so that you can model how to use it.

3. With children's help, choose a familiar object or animal. Write its name at the top of the graphic organizer. Some ideas you might suggest include a pencil, a puppy, an ice cube, an ice cream cone, a strawberry, a rainbow, or a snowflake.

4. Invite children to think of details about the object or animal that might give a clue about it. Review the list of clue details, choose three, and put checks beside them.

5. With children, write clues based on each detail chosen. To help generate hints, position the clue details as questions, such as "What does it look like? What does it do? What does it sound like? Where might people see it?"

6. On a separate sheet of chart paper, put your clues together to write the riddle.

7. On the same day or during another session, revisit your riddle poem and remind children of the steps they took to write it. Then give them a fresh copy of the organizer. Following the same techniques used above, help children use the organizer to plan their own riddle poems. When you feel children are ready, have them write their poems on a separate sheet of paper. Invite children to read their finished riddles aloud for classmates to solve.

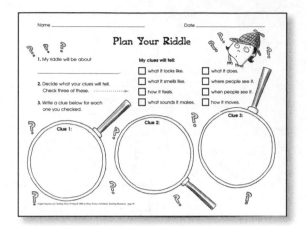

POETRY TIP

Although many riddle poems rhyme, it is important that children focus more on creating useful hints than on matching sounds. If the clues come easily, however, you may want to help children experiment with rhyme to enhance their riddle poems.

Name _____

Date _____

Plan Your Riddle

1. My riddle will be about _____

2. Decide what your clues will tell.
   Check three of these.

3. Write a clue below for each one you checked.

My clues will tell:

☐ what it looks like.

☐ what it smells like.

☐ how it feels.

☐ what sounds it makes.

☐ what it does.

☐ where people see it.

☐ when people see it.

☐ how it moves.

Clue 1:

Clue 2:

Clue 3:

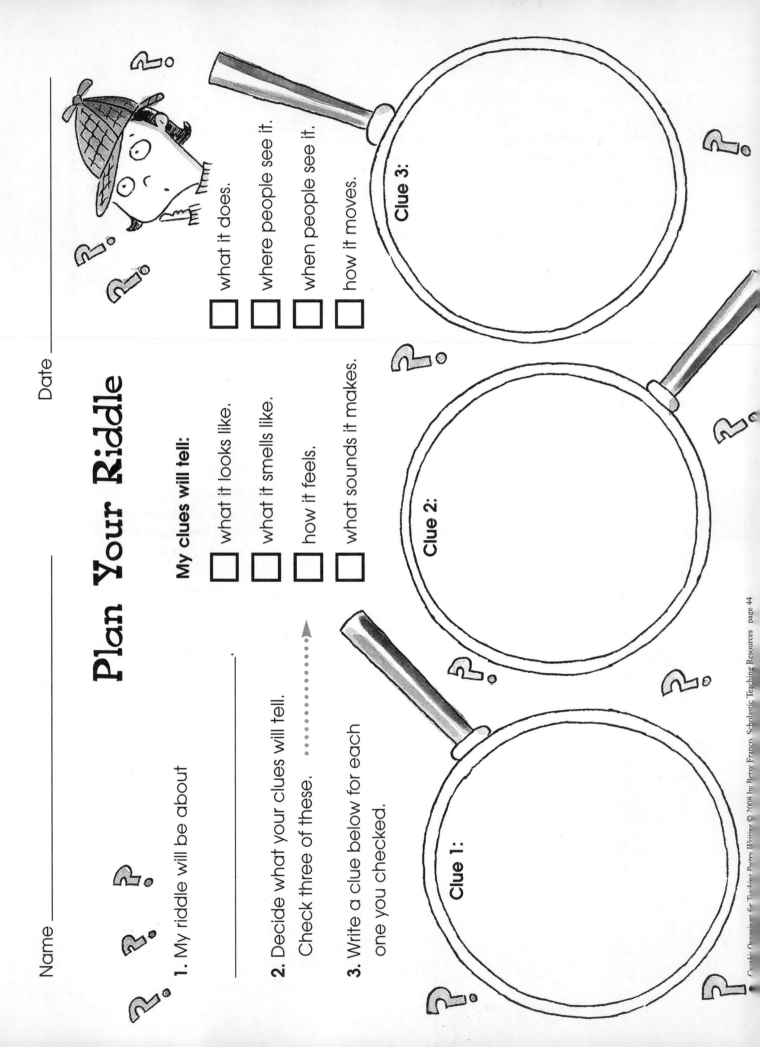

Ode to Pizza

Your melted cheese,
so smooth
and thick,
makes golden threads
that glisten and stick.

Your pepperoni
in chunk after chunk
adds circles of spice
with extra spunk.

Your crust that crunches
crisp and loud
is puffy inside
like a cumulus cloud.

Oh, luscious pizza,
I don't think twice.
I always gobble
slice after slice!

Writing an Ode

Activate Prior Knowledge

Invite children to list some positive feelings, such as feeling happy, loving, excited, proud, and grateful. Explain that when people like someone or something very much, they usually feel this way for a reason. Perhaps they love a dog because it is warm, loving, and playful. They might like ice cream because it tastes sweet and feels cool and smooth.

Share the Poem

1. Tell children that today's poem is called an *ode*, a poem in which the writer shares feelings about someone or something that he or she really likes or loves.

2. Show children only the title of the poem. Read the title aloud, and ask them to tell some wonderful things they enjoy about pizza.

3. Distribute copies of the poem (page 45), write it on chart paper, or copy it onto an overhead transparency.

4. Read the poem aloud once and then a second time with children. Ask: "How does this poet feel about pizza? What parts of the poem tell you that?"

5. Point out that in this poem the writer describes parts of the pizza by comparing it to other things, saying, for example, that the melted cheese makes "golden threads," and the crust is as "puffy" as a "cloud." By comparing the pizza in this way, the poet gives the reader a vivid picture of what he or she has in mind. The poet is able to describe it well in just a few words.

6. Point out that in keeping with the form of an ode, the writer is speaking to the pizza, just as he or she might tell her feelings to a person.

Scaffold Using the Graphic Organizer

1. Explain to children that they will be writing their own odes. First, you will write one together.

2. Photocopy and distribute the graphic organizer (page 48). If possible, copy the organizer onto an overhead transparency or enlarge it so that you can model how to use it.

3. As a class, choose a food to write your ode about. Try to choose a food that many students like, such as macaroni and cheese, chocolate chip cookies, or bubble gum ice cream. Write its name at the top of the organizer.

4. Ask children to close their eyes and picture the food in their minds. Encourage them to remember what the food looks, smells, and tastes like, and why they like it so much.

5. Have children open their eyes and talk aloud to the food, as if it were there in the room with them. Use the organizer to write down what they say. Encourage them to describe their food by comparing it to whatever it reminds them of.

6. Help children number the ideas in the order they want to write about them. As a class, write the ode in that order on a sheet of chart paper.

7. On the same day or during another session, revisit your ode and remind children of the steps they took to write it. Then give them a fresh copy of the organizer. Following the same techniques used above, help children use the organizer to plan their own odes. When you feel children are ready, have them write their poems on a separate sheet of paper. Then have them illustrate their odes and attach the poems to the pictures.

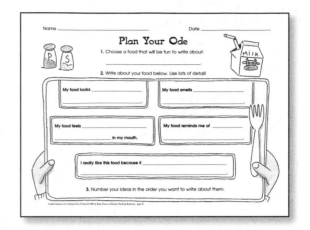

POETRY TIP

Odes are highly effective when the poet relies on simile and metaphor to paint a vivid picture with words. Simile occurs when the writer uses "like" or "as" to compare two items, as in *The sun glowed like a ball of fire*. Metaphor involves the writer actually saying that the subject *is* another item, as in *The cloud is a pillow under my head*.

Name _____

Date _____

Plan Your Ode

1. Choose a food that will be fun to write about:

_____

2. Write about your food below. Use lots of detail!

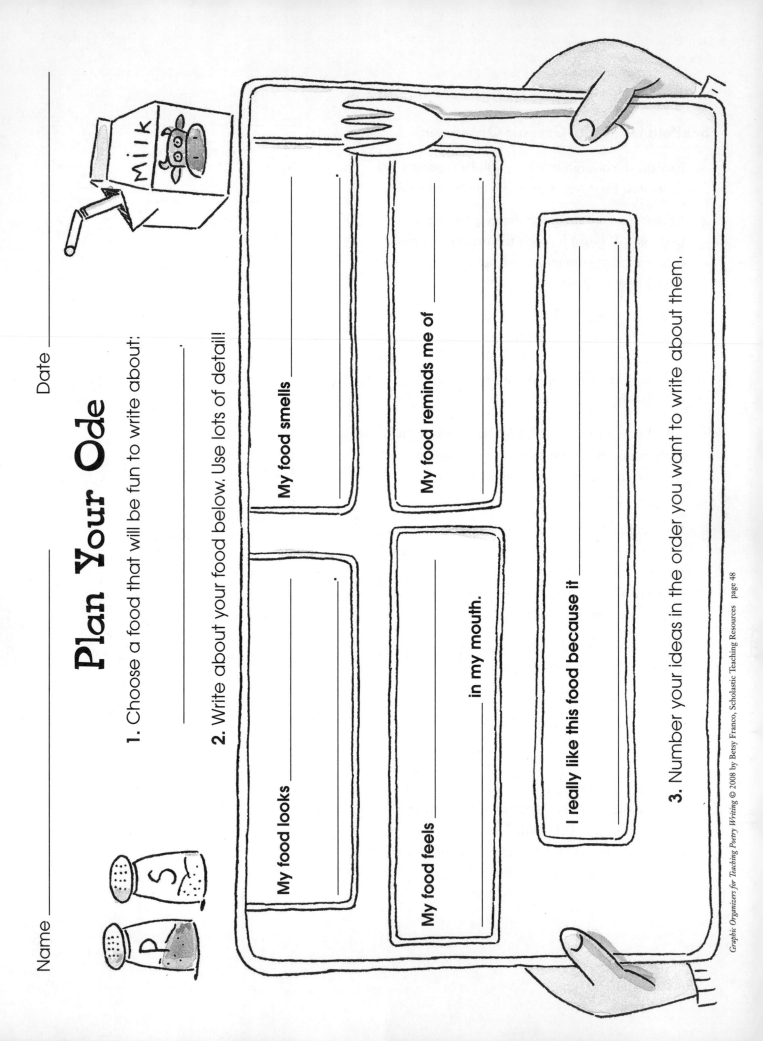

My food looks _____

My food smells _____

My food feels _____ in my mouth.

My food reminds me of _____

I really like this food because it _____

3. Number your ideas in the order you want to write about them.

Skateboard Rap

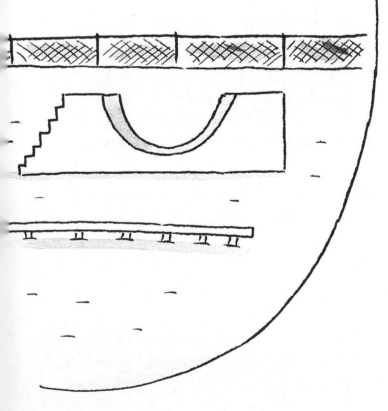

My board and I
see eye to eye.
We rip the ramps.
We burn.
We fly.

We're champions
of the skateboard world.
We outride
any boy or girl.
We whirl.
We twirl.
We launch.
We swirl.

We tear the air.
Don't have a care.
A daring pair—
got speed and flair.

A hawk in flight,
we're out of sight.
We land just right
all day or night.

A perfect double,
we don't make trouble.
You watch us go,
put on a show.

Hey, don't you know?
From head to toe,
our moves are sweet.
We can't be beat!

Writing a Rap Poem

Activate Prior Knowledge

Write the word *rap* on the chalkboard. Invite children to tell what they know about rap—what it is, and where they have heard it before.

Share the Poem

1. Distribute copies of the poem (page 49), write it on chart paper, or copy it onto an overhead transparency.

2. Explain to students that the poem they are about to hear and read is a *rap poem*. Then read the poem aloud once, following its rhythm.

3. Read the poem aloud a second time and move a little as you read, nodding your head and bobbing your body slightly. Invite children to move along with you, feeling the rhythm of the poem in their bodies.

4. Explain that rap poems depend on rhythm, which is the flow of sound. In a rap poem, much of the rhythm is repetitive; it makes a pattern with sound.

5. Read the poem aloud again while children listen. Invite them to tell where the rhythm changes and where it repeats. Point out that much of the poem reads in beats of four. Tap out the beats on a drum or desktop.

6. Ask children what else they notice about the poem other than its rhythm—its rhyme! Explain that in rap poems, writers try to include as many rhymes as possible. Use a highlighting marker to identify the rhyming words in the poem as children name them.

7. Finally, talk about the idea that rap poems are often "bragging" poems, in which the writer exaggerates some talent he or she has, like riding a skateboard.

Scaffold Using the Graphic Organizer

1. Explain to children that they will be writing their own rap poems. First, you will write one together.

2. Photocopy and distribute the graphic organizer (page 52). If possible, copy the organizer onto an overhead transparency or enlarge it so that you can model how to use it.

3. Help children think of a topic for the class rap poem. Ask: "What is something our class is really good at or something we really enjoy doing? What can we can brag about?" Write that topic at the top of the organizer.

4. Invite children to brag about themselves. Brainstorm a list of words and phrases words that go with your topic. Write these on the lines above the skateboards.

5. Ask children to think of groups of rhyming words that go with your topic (They don't have to be perfect rhymes; close ones are good enough.) List each group inside a skateboard.

6. Have children number the groups in the order they want to mention them in the poem. Then help them create the poem on a separate sheet of chart paper. Encourage them to keep the lines short.

7. On the same day or during another session, revisit your rap poem and remind children of the steps they took to create it. Then give them a fresh copy of the organizer. Following the same techniques used above, help children use the organizer to plan their own rap poems. When you feel children are ready, have them write their poems on a separate sheet of paper. Encourage children to write short lines and lots of rhymes, and above all, have fun!

Name _____ Date _____

Plan Your Rap Poem

1. Write about something you do well. I am really good at _____
2. On the lines below, brag about how good you are.
3. On the skateboards, list groups of rhyming words that go with your topic.

POETRY TIPS

* For this poem, guide children to choose activities that involve lots of action such as gymnastics, kickball, dancing, singing, playing a musical instrument, building or fixing things, or making friends. These choices are more likely to suggest enough action words to make an effective rap poem.

* Prepare children for rhyming by reviewing word families that will provide them with ample choices for matching words that rhyme.

Kickball Rap

Taj kicks the ball
over the wall.
It flies up high
touching the sky!

Jaileen runs past
the bases fast.
The kids yell, "Wow!
Run to Home now!"

Singing Rap

When our class sings
the whole room rings.
With voices strong,
we belt out a song.

We trill.
We thrill.
We hum.
We stun!

When we croon a tune,
the birds all swoon!

Name _____

Date _____

Plan Your Rap Poem

1. Write about something you do well. I am really good at _____

2. On the lines below, brag about how good you are.

_____

_____

3. On the skateboards, list groups of rhyming words that go with your topic.

A Frog Talking to a Kid Who's Trying to Catch Him

With toes pointed and my rubbery
skin stretched to the max
I spring and leap and spring and leap just
out of your reach until I hit the pond

SPLISH!

AND WHISH!

I get away . . . .

Time to Come Out

Turtle, turtle!
Come out. Come out.
You don't have to play
hide and seek!
It's safe to come out
and take a peek.

Writing a Concrete Poem

Activate Prior Knowledge

Draw a four-inch circle on an overhead transparency. Cover the circle with a blank transparency to form an overlay. Ask children to identify the shape they see (*a circle*). Then ask them to describe a circle in a sentence or two, such as "A circle is a shape that goes around and around." and "It does not start or stop." On the overlay, write the sentence(s) inside the circle so that they take its shape. Then remove the bottom transparency, leaving only the circle-shaped sentences on display. Ask children what shape the words have made. Help them connect the idea that the words tell about a circle and they also form the shape of a circle.

A circle is a shape that goes around and around. It does not start or stop.

Share the Poem

1. Tell children that they will be reading poems that are shaped like what they tell about. Explain that this type of poem is called a *concrete poem*.

2. Distribute copies of the concrete poems (page 53), or copy them onto an overhead transparency.

3. Read the frog poem together. Then talk about its shape. Invite children to tell why the poet arranged the words to look like a frog hopping (*because the poem tells about a frog hopping*). Point out that the poem is not very long, making it easy to read, to understand, and to connect to the image.

4. Repeat this discussion for the second poem, which tells about a turtle hiding in its shell. Help children compare the arrangement of the words in this poem with that of the frog poem. (In the turtle poem, the poet placed the words inside the shape to create the form of a turtle. Explain that this is another way to create a concrete poem.

Scaffold Using the Graphic Organizer

1. Tell children that they will be writing their own concrete poems. First, you will write one together.

2. Photocopy and distribute the graphic organizer (page 56). If possible, copy the organizer onto an overhead transparency or enlarge it so that you can model how to use it.

3. With children's help, choose an animal or familiar object that will be easy to draw. Write its name inside the small frame on the graphic organizer. Then draw a simple sketch of the object or item inside the large frame. Ideas for simple drawings might include a mouse, a balloon, a kite, or a mountain. (Later, independently, children may wish to draw more complex drawings of animals in motion, such as a bird flying.)

4. Invite children to help you write a simple poem that tells about the animal or object you have drawn. Write the words inside the shape, filling it as best you can and placing the words as needed to follow its shape.

5. On the same day or during another session, revisit your concrete poem and remind children of the steps they took to write it. Then give them a fresh copy of the organizer. Following the same techniques used above, help children use the organizer to plan their own concrete poems. Encourage them to choose topics that lend themselves to simple drawings with few curves or angles, such as a house, a lunch box or a ball. Remind them that their drawings should be basic and easy to fill with words. When you feel children are ready, have them copy their poems onto a separate sheet of paper.

Name _____ Date _____

Plan Your Concrete Poem

1. My poem will be about
2. Draw a picture of its shape inside the frame below.
3. Now write about your picture. Write the words inside the shape.

Name _____   Date _____

Plan Your Concrete Poem

1. My poem will be about

_____ .

2. Draw a picture of its shape inside the frame below.

3. Now write about your picture. Write the words inside the shape.

Walking Home in a Storm

To the beat of the wind,
the trees dance and sway.
The rain seeps down
my raincoat neck,
dripping, dropping
every which way.

I smell the earth all soggy wet.
A boom!
A slash!
A lightning flash!
I scurry along
and slip and trip.

But then I stop
and enjoy each drop.
I taste a raindrop on my cheek.
It's salty and it's kind of sweet.

I let myself get wonderfully wet
and I jump in the
next . . .
big . . .
PUDDLE!

Writing a Senses Poem

Activate Prior Knowledge

Hold up one hand, and ask children to tell how many fingers they see. Then ask them to tell how many senses we have. Point to each finger as you help children name each of the five senses: *seeing*, *hearing*, *smelling*, *touching*, and *tasting*. Write each sense on chart paper, an overhead transparency, or the chalkboard. Point to each one and ask: "What can we (see/hear/smell/ touch/taste)?" Write children's responses beside each sense. For example, they might say they can see flowers, colors, and clouds. They might say they can smell pizza, perfume, and mowed grass. (Hint: Watch for connections. For example, children may say that they can see flowers, and they can also smell and touch them as well.)

Share the Poem

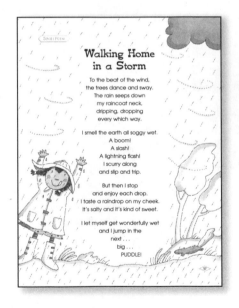

1. Explain to children that poetry depends on the senses. The more a poet tells about the way something feels, smells, tastes, and so on, the better the reader is able to experience it. Point out that some poems are written exactly for that reason: to help the reader see, hear, touch, taste, or smell, or all of these at once.

2. Tell children that you are going to share a *senses poem*. Distribute copies of the poem (page 57), write it on chart paper, or copy it onto an overhead transparency. Read the poem aloud and then invite the class to read along with you.

3. Invite students to look over the poem and choose at least one phrase that describes each of the senses:

seeing:	". . . the trees dance and sway." and "A lightning flash!"
hearing:	"A boom!"
smelling:	"I smell the earth all soggy wet."
tasting:	"It's salty and it's kind of sweet."
touching/ feeling:	"The rain seeps down my raincoat neck, dripping, dropping every which way."

Scaffold Using the Graphic Organizer

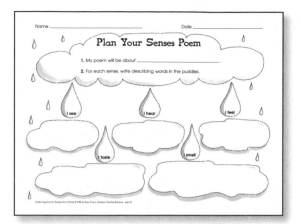

1. Tell children that the class will plan and write a senses poem. With children's help, choose a topic that is rich in sensory details, such as swimming in a pool or the ocean, going to a baseball game, attending a street fair, or watching a parade.

2. Photocopy and distribute the graphic organizer (page 60). If possible, copy the organizer onto an overhead transparency or enlarge it so that you can model how to use it.

3. Write the topic of the poem on the line at the top of the graphic organizer. For each sense, brainstorm words to describe the topic. Ask: "What do you see? What do you smell? What sounds do you hear?" and so on. For example, *pungent* might describe a smell at a street fair. Write the words in the corresponding puddle on the organizer.

4. On a separate sheet of chart paper or overhead, help children use the describing words to write sentences, such as "The pungent odors of cooking food float by."

5. Help children use their sentences to create a senses poem that makes the reader feel as though he or she is right there with them—seeing, hearing, smelling, tasting, and touching what they describe.

6. On the same day or during another session, revisit your senses poem and remind children of the steps they took to write it. Then give them a fresh copy of the organizer. Following the same techniques used above, help children use the organizer to plan their own senses poems. When you feel children are ready, have them write their poems on a separate sheet of paper.

POETRY TIPS

★ Remind children that the clouds and raindrops on the organizer will simply help them identify and organize their ideas—their poems can be on any topic of their choosing.

★ Emphasize the idea that the sentences children write on the organizer don't have to be the same as the ones in their poems. The organizer is meant to help children develop ideas and structure for the poem. Your writers can and should feel free to make changes as they write.

Name _____

Date _____

Plan Your Senses Poem

1. My poem will be about _____

2. For each sense, write describing words in the puddles.

I feel

I smell

I hear

I see

I taste

Teddy Bear

Tummy as snuggly as a pillow.

Eyes like ripe berries in the fall.

Dappled with stains.

Definitely huggable.

You're falling apart.

But don't worry,

Even if your insides seep out

And the thread holding in your eyes unravels, you'll still

Reign as the queen of my stuffed animals.

Writing an Acrostic Poem

Activate Prior Knowledge

Write the word *across* for children to see. Ask them to tell what the word means. Explain that when we write sentences, the words go across the page.

Share the Poem

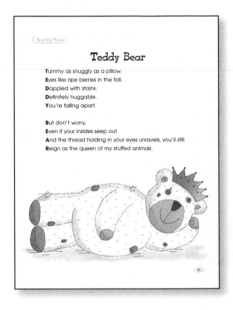

1. Distribute copies of the poem (page 61), write it on chart paper, or copy it onto an overhead transparency.

2. Invite children to tell what they notice about the poem (*the first letter on each line is darker than the rest; the dark letters spell* teddy bear *and are written vertically down the page*).

3. Tell children that this type of poem is called an *acrostic*. Each line of an acrostic starts with a letter that becomes the first letter of a word, phrase, or sentence. Usually, the words that go across tell something about the word (or words) formed by the first letter of each line.

4. Read the poem together. Discuss vocabulary words that may be unfamiliar.

5. Help children notice that the first verse tells how the teddy bear looks and feels. It compares the teddy bear to other objects (using simile): *Tummy as snuggly as a pillow. Eyes like ripe berries in the fall.*

6. Point out that in the second verse, the lines form one long sentence that tells how the poet feels about the teddy bear.

Scaffold Using the Graphic Organizer

1. Tell children that they will be writing their own acrostics. First, you will write one together.

2. Photocopy and distribute the graphic organizer (page 64). If possible, copy the organizer onto an overhead transparency or enlarge it so that you can model how to use it.

3. With children's help, choose a subject for your poem. This may be the name of a familiar object, animal, or person. Write the name on the line at the top of the graphic organizer.

4. Write each letter of the name in its own block on the organizer. (Leave extra blocks empty.) Then invite children to help you think of a word that begins with that letter. Point to the first line of the teddy bear poem to help them recall that the letter *T* started the word *tummy*, a part of the teddy bear's body.

5. Ask children to think of a sentence or phrase that goes with the first word they wrote. In the teddy bear poem, the poet went beyond just naming the word tummy. She described it and wrote "Tummy as snuggly as a pillow."

6. Once the poem is complete, reread it several times with children. Remind them again that the first letter on each line works with the others to spell a word. Each line of the poem tells something about the poem's subject. That is the goal of writing an acrostic—to write a poem based on the letters that spell the name of an object, animal, or person.

7. On the same day or during another session, revisit your acrostic and remind children of the steps they took to write it. Then give them a fresh copy of the organizer. Following the same techniques used above, help children use the organizer to plan their own acrostic. When you feel children are ready, have them copy their acrostic poems onto a separate sheet of paper.

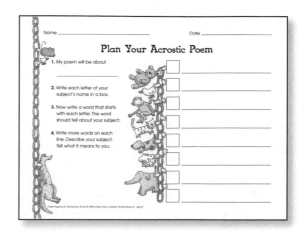

POETRY TIPS

* The organizer has room for words containing up to eight letters. For longer words, give children another copy of the organizer. Children can tape the pages together so that the boxes on the pages line up.

* Children may enjoy writing an acrostic about a favorite stuffed animal. Before teaching the lesson, invite children to bring one to school. Have extras on hand for children who may not be able to bring one in.

Name _____

Date _____

Plan Your Acrostic Poem

1. My poem will be about _____

2. Write each letter of your subject's name in a box.

3. Now write a word that starts with each letter. The word should tell about your subject.

4. Write more words on each line. Describe your subject. Tell what it means to you.

Why?

Why can't my birthday
be 12 times a year?
Why can't my chores
just all disappear?
Why can't school
get out at noon?
Why can't my pet
be an owl or raccoon?
Why can't I have
my very own room?
Why can't I zip
around on a broom?
Why can't I be
a wizard or king?
Then I could change
all of those things!

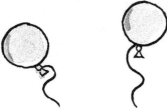

Writing a Question Poem

Activate Prior Knowledge

Ask: "What is a question?" Explain that a question is a sentence that asks for information. When people want to know something, they usually ask a question. Invite children to make up questions they might ask a friend, such as "How are you feeling today?" or "Would you like to play soccer with me?"

Share the Poem

1. Distribute copies of the poem (page 65), write it on chart paper, or copy it onto an overhead transparency.

2. Explain that today's poem is called a *question poem*. Invite children to tell why it has that name.

3. Read the poem aloud. Then invite children to read it with you.

4. Have children identify the wishes in the poem that could really happen (*chores disappearing, school getting out early, having an owl for a pet, having ones' own room*) and the ones that are fantasy or make pretend (*becoming a wizard, zipping around on a broom, and having twelve birthdays a year*).

Scaffold Using the Graphic Organizer

1. Tell children that they will be writing their own question poems. First you will write one together.

2. Photocopy and distribute the graphic organizer (page 68). If possible, copy the organizer onto an overhead transparency or enlarge it so that you can model how to use it.

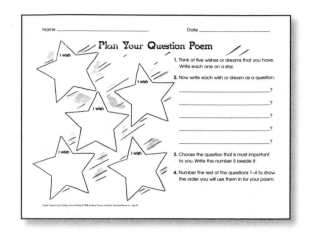

3. Ask children to take a moment to think about some wishes and dreams that they have. List these on chart paper as children name them. Ask children to tell you which wishes are real and which are fantasy. Circle those that are real; underline those that are fantasy.

4. Invite children to choose five wishes and/or dreams from the list. Write each on a star on the graphic organizer. Then tell children to phrase them as questions, imitating the style of the question poem. Write these on the graphic organizer. Then number the questions in the order that children want them to appear in the poem. Encourage them to save a special question for last to end the poem.

5. On the same day or during another session, revisit your question poem and remind children of the steps they took to create it. Then give them a fresh copy of the organizer. Ask them to use the questions they see on the list they made earlier—or new ones they come up with—to plan their own question poems. When you feel children are ready, have them write their poems on a separate sheet of paper.

Name _____

Date _____

Plan Your Question Poem

1. Think of five wishes or dreams that you have. Write each one on a star.

2. Now write each wish or dream as a question.

_____ ?

_____ ?

_____ ?

_____ ?

_____ ?

3. Choose the question that is most important to you. Write the number 5 beside it.

4. Number the rest of the questions 1–4 to show the order you will use them in for your poem.

I wish

I wish

I wish

I wish

I wish

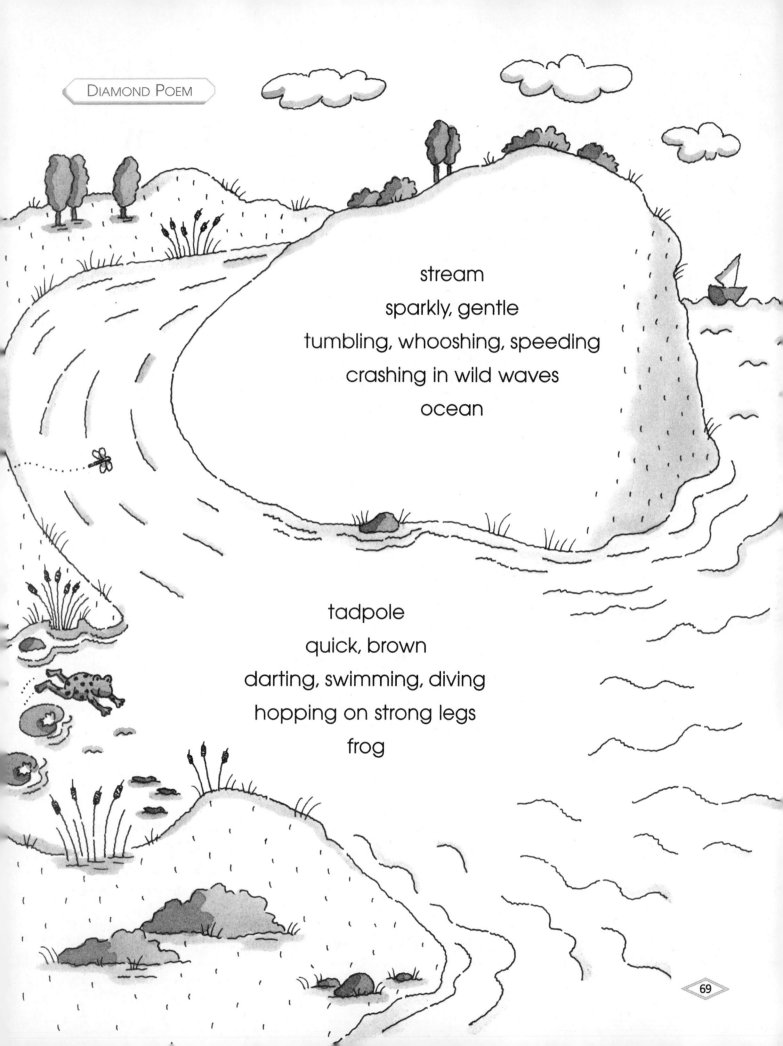

stream
sparkly, gentle
tumbling, whooshing, speeding
crashing in wild waves
ocean

tadpole
quick, brown
darting, swimming, diving
hopping on strong legs
frog

Writing a Diamond Poem

Activate Prior Knowledge

Show children a pattern block in the shape of a diamond, also known as a rhombus. Ask them to identify the shape. Point out that it is narrow at the top and bottom and wider in the middle.

Share the Poem

1. Distribute copies of the poems (page 69), write them on chart paper, or copy onto an overhead transparency.

2. Ask children to look at the first poem and tell what shape they see (*a diamond*).

3. Read the first poem aloud. Then read it together.

4. With children's help, count the number of lines in the poem (*five*). Explain that each of the five lines has a job. The jobs are as follows:

   Line one contains a naming word. It tells what the poem is about.

   Line two contains two describing words. They describe the naming word.

   Line three contains three action words. They tell what the naming word does.

   Line four tells how the first naming word is growing or changing in some way.

   Line five contains one naming word. It tells what the first naming word has become.

5. Reread the first poem. Ask children to tell what the poem talks about at the beginning (*a stream*) and what it becomes at the end (*the ocean*). Help them identify where in the poem the poet describes a stream and tells what it does. Then ask them where the poet tells how the stream changes into an ocean (*line four*).

6. Repeat the process for the second diamond poem, about a tadpole's growth into a frog.

Scaffold Using the Graphic Organizer

1. Tell children that the class will plan and write a diamond poem. As a class, brainstorm living or nonliving things that undergo changes and become something else, such as a raindrop that turns into a storm or a caterpillar that transforms into a butterfly. Choose one that you will use to demonstrate how to organize and write a diamond poem.

2. Photocopy and distribute the graphic organizer (page 72). If possible, copy the organizer onto an overhead transparency or enlarge it so that you can model how to use it.

◇ Direct children's attention to the kite organizer.

◇ On line one, write the word that will start your poem, for example, *caterpillar*.

> On line five, write the word that will end your poem, for example, *butterfly*.

◇ On line two, write two words that describe the word on line one (for example, *striped, fuzzy*).

◇ On line three, write three action words that tell what the named object or living thing is doing (for example, *munching, growing, hiding*).

◇ Use line four to indicate that changes are happening (for example, *wiggling wet wings*).

> Reread your poem and then take out or add words as needed in order to keep a diamond shape.

3. On the same day or during another session, revisit your diamond poem and remind children of the steps they took to create it. Then give them a fresh copy of the organizer. Following the same techniques used above, help children use the organizer to plan their own diamond poems. When you feel children are ready, have them copy their poems onto a separate sheet of paper.

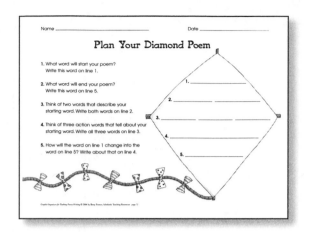

POETRY TIP

Ideas for Diamond Poems:
- rumble/earthquake
- breeze/storm
- seed/flower
- egg/chick
- rock/sand

Plan Your Diamond Poem

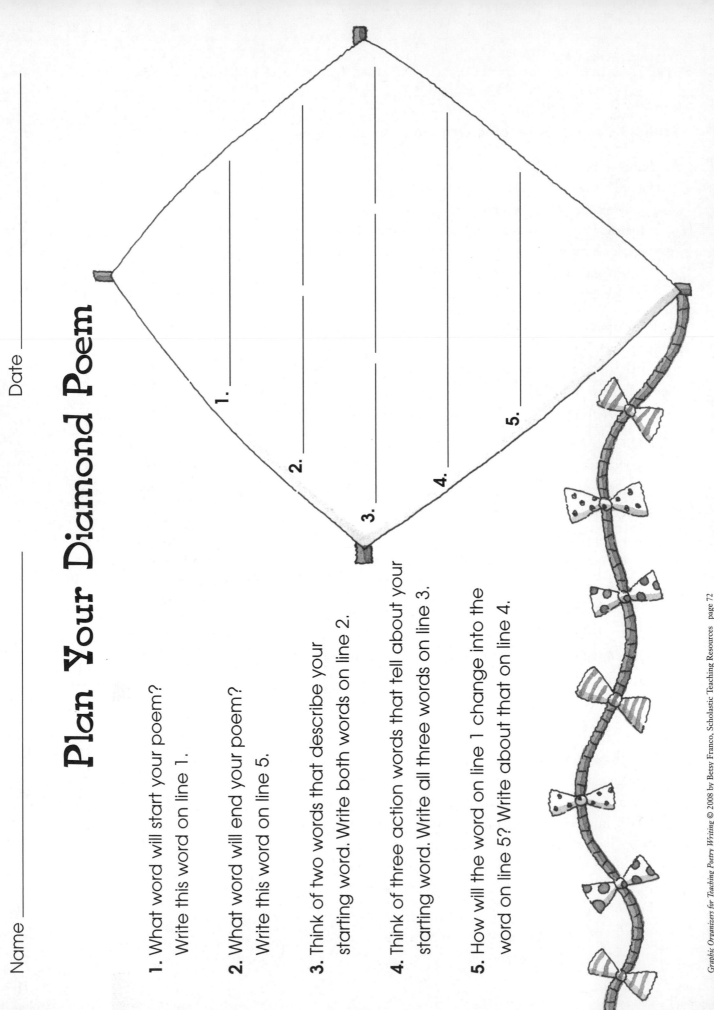

1. _____

2. _____

3. _____

4. _____

5. _____

1. What word will start your poem? Write this word on line 1.

2. What word will end your poem? Write this word on line 5.

3. Think of two words that describe your starting word. Write both words on line 2.

4. Think of three action words that tell about your starting word. Write all three words on line 3.

5. How will the word on line 1 change into the word on line 5? Write about that on line 4.

I Remember

I was five years old in
the department store
scurrying from one rack
of clothes to another
like a mouse in
the bushes
until I came out and I
was
Lost
LOST
LOST!
Faces, arms, legs
going by
Not my dad
NOT my dad
NOT MY DAD
Uh-oh
Alone
ALONE
ALL ALONE

Then
DAD!
MY DAD!
HUGGING ME TIGHT!
HUGGING ME TIGHT!

73

Writing a Memory Poem

Activate Prior Knowledge

Ask children to close their eyes and remember something exciting that happened to them recently. Help them realize that thoughts of what happened in the past are called memories. As time permits, invite several volunteers to share their memories with the class.

Share the Poem

1. Distribute copies of the poem (page 73), write it on chart paper, or copy it onto an overhead transparency.

2. Explain that today's poem is called a *memory poem*. It is a poem that tells a story about something that really happened—something that the poet remembers and that has made an impression. Read the poem aloud once and then again as children read with you.

3. Have children retell what happened in the poem.

4. Ask: "How did the poet feel about this memory?" (*scared and relieved*) "How can you tell?" (*She described an event that would be scary for a five-year-old. She expressed her fear by repeating and enlarging words words such as "Lost," "Not my dad," and "Alone." She expressed relief by shouting "DAD! MY DAD!" in capital letters.*)

5. Explain that most memories do bring out feelings—be they happy, sad, frightened, or embarrassed. Talk about the ways that poets can use and change words to show the reader how they feel: by repeating words, making the letters larger or capitalizing them, and adding italics and exclamation marks.

Scaffold Using the Graphic Organizer

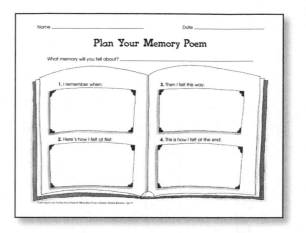

1. Tell children that the class will plan and write a memory poem. Together, choose an event that the class experienced together and remembers quite well, such as a field trip or recent class activity. Steer children away from describing unpleasant encounters between classmates.

2. Photocopy and distribute the graphic organizer (page 76). If possible, copy the organizer onto an overhead transparency or enlarge it so that you can model how to use it.

3. Write the topic of the memory at the top of the organizer. Then ask children to close their eyes and recall what happened. When they open their eyes, ask them to help you reconstruct the event on the organizer, writing what happened and in what order.

4. Use the information on the organizer to retell the story in poem form.

5. On the same day or during another session, revisit your memory poem and remind children of the steps they took to create it. Then give them a fresh copy of the organizer. Following the same techniques used above, have children recall details about a single event in their own lives, record the details on their organizer, and then use the organizer as a guide for creating their memory poems. When you feel children are ready, have them write their poems on a separate sheet of paper.

Name _____

Plan Your Memory Poem

What memory will you tell about? _____

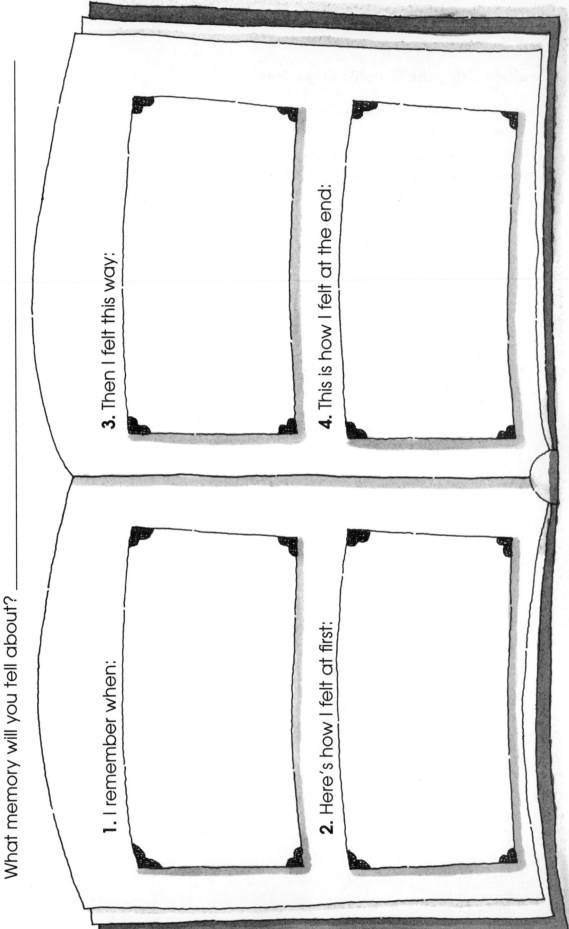

1. I remember when:

2. Here's how I felt at first:

3. Then I felt this way:

4. This is how I felt at the end:

Limerick

There once was a puppy named Pat
who adored every kitty cat.
    He would lick the cats clean
    as his morning routine.
All the dogs teased him *badly* for that!

A lady who didn't like light
and thought that the day was too bright
    found a bat and raccoon
    by the light of the moon
and she helped them both hunt every night.

A gentleman strolled along
with his cat on a leash that was strong.
    The cat had a fit,
    didn't like it one bit,
though the leash was a hundred feet long.

Writing a Limerick

Activate Prior Knowledge

Ask children to tell you what they think a *limerick* is and invite them to recite any portions of a limerick they might remember. Explain that a limerick is a fun poem that tells about an animal or person who is usually silly or unusual in some way.

Share the Poem

1. Distribute copies of the limericks (page 77), write them on chart paper, or copy onto an overhead transparency.

2. Explain that today you will share three limericks. Read the first limerick aloud once. Then invite children to read it along with you.

3. Ask children to tell who is the star (or main character) of the limerick (*a puppy named Pat*). Then invite them to talk about Pat's behavior in the poem. Ask: "Is Pat acting the way a puppy normally would? Why do you say that? How do the other dogs react to Pat licking the cats clean every morning? Why do you think they are acting this way?"

4. Explain that most limericks are about silly ways that people or animals act. They are meant to entertain people and make them laugh.

5. Explain that part of what makes a limerick so much fun to read and to write is its rhythm and rhyme. Read the limerick again. This time, clap to its rhythm and invite children to clap, too. Then have children use crayons or highlighting markers to underline the rhyming words in the limerick.

6. Repeat the process for the two remaining limericks.

Scaffold Using the Graphic Organizer

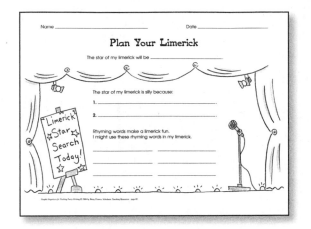

1. Tell children that the class will plan and write a limerick. Together, choose an animal or person that can easily be imagined in a silly way, such as a monkey, an ant, or a bug. (Keep rhyming possibilities in mind as you help students brainstorm; it's easy to find words that rhyme with simple words such as *ant*, *bug*, and *pig*.)

2. Photocopy and distribute the graphic organizer (page 80.) If possible, copy the organizer onto an overhead transparency or enlarge it so that you can model how to use it.

3. Identify the subject of the limerick by writing the person's or animal's name at the top of the organizer, beside "The star of my limerick will be _____."

4. Work with children to write two examples of the star's silly behavior, such as "He likes to sleep upside-down," or "She never ate anything cold."

5. Create a list of words that are easy to rhyme with. Write these on the graphic organizer.

6. Revisit the limericks on the poetry page to help children recall their rhythm and to show how a character might be introduced.

7. On a separate sheet of chart paper, help children use what you have written on the organizer to create a limerick together. Start by introducing the person or animal "star" of the poem. Then move through the process of writing a limerick, telling of silly or unusual behaviors and using words that rhyme.

8. On the same day or during another session, revisit your limerick and remind children of the steps they took to create it. Then give them a fresh copy of the organizer. Following the same techniques used above, help children use the organizer to plan their own limericks. When you feel children are ready, have them write their limericks on a separate sheet of paper.

POETRY TIP

Because a limerick has a strong beat, it is a good poetry form to use with children who are auditory learners.

Name _____

Date _____

Plan Your Limerick

The star of my limerick will be _____

The star of my limerick is silly because:

1. _____

2. _____

Rhyming words make a limerick fun.
I might use these rhyming words in my limerick.

_____

_____

_____

_____

Limerick ☆ Star ☆ Search! ☆ Today!

Sssssounds of Summer

clackity-clack,
clackity-clack.
My scooter on the sidewalk squares

ga-lump, ga-lump,
ga-lump, ga-lump.
A soda in my pack somewhere.

flap-a-flap-a-flap-a-flap.
A leaf caught in my bicycle spoke.

frrrrr-fer-rip, frrrrr-fer-rip.
The neighbor's sprinkler!

LET'S GET SOAKED!

Writing a Sound Poem

Activate Prior Knowledge

Have everyone sit quietly and listen to the sounds around them. Have them list the sounds, such as *vroooooon* for a city bus going past your school or *boing, boing* for a ball bouncing on the playground. Make a list of the sounds they hear.

Share the Poem

1. Distribute copies of the poem (page 81), write it on chart paper, or copy it onto an overhead transparency.

2. Explain that today you will share a poem that is all about sounds. Talk about the title. Ask: "What do you notice about the first word?" *(The "s" in the word* sounds *is repeated.)*

3. Read the poem aloud, and then have children read the poem with you.

4. Ask children to find all the sounds in the poem and repeat them aloud. Then ask them to list other sounds they might hear in the summer. Encourage them to make up words that capture those sounds.

Scaffold Using the Graphic Organizer

1. Tell children that the class will plan and write a sound poem. Together, choose a topic for the group of sounds you will write about, such as sounds of an amusement park, sounds of a zoo, or sounds of weather or a season, such as spring.

2. Photocopy and distribute the graphic organizer (page 84). If possible, copy the organizer onto an overhead transparency or enlarge it so that you can model how to use it.

3. Write the topic of the poem at the top of the organizer.

4. Have children close their eyes and "hear" the sounds associated with the topic. Ask them to name the source of the sounds. If the topic is a spring rainstorm, for example, they might name the sound of rain on a roof, wind in the trees, and thunder. On each of the solid lines, write the name of an animal, person, or thing that makes each sound.

5. With children's help, make up a word to describe each exact sound, for example, "Plippity-plip-PLOP!" for the rain, "Whooooosh-swooosh!!" for the wind, and "Rumble-THWACK!" for thunder. Write these words on the corresponding dotted lines coming out of the sprinkler. Children can invent words—so anything goes!

6. Enlist children's help in numbering the sounds in the order they want them to appear in the poem. Tell them to choose the most interesting or unusual sound for last.

7. Put the sounds together to create a poem in the style of "Sssssounds of Summer." When writing the poem, repeat each made-up sound word twice. Then write beneath it what causes that sound.

8. On the same day or during another session, revisit your sound poem and remind children of the steps they took to create it. Then give them a fresh copy of the organizer. Following the same techniques used above, help children use the organizer to plan their own sound poems. When you feel children are ready, have them write their poems on a separate sheet of paper.

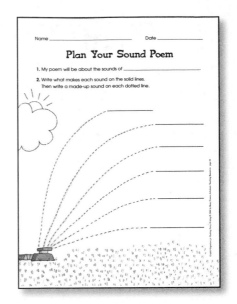

Name _____ Date _____

Plan Your Sound Poem

1. My poem will be about the sounds of _____

2. Write what makes each sound on the solid lines.
   Then write a made-up sound on each dotted line.

POETRY TIP

Warm up children's listening skills by asking them to listen closely to specific sounds of nature or sounds around the school and describe them in words. If possible, you might record routine, familiar sounds such as water running, a child brushing his teeth, a dog barking, someone hammering, and so on. Let children listen to the sounds and identify their sources.

Plan Your Sound Poem

1. My poem will be about the sounds of _____.

2. Write what makes each sound on the solid lines.
   Then write a made-up sound on each dotted line.

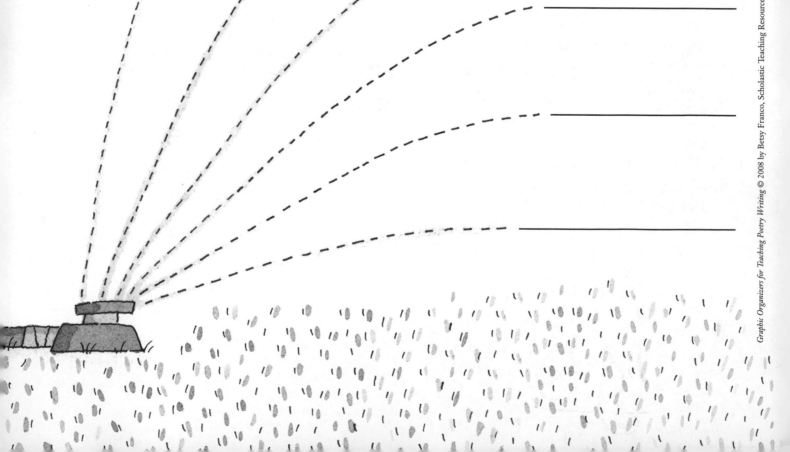

Why I Didn't Get My Homework Done

I didn't get my homework done,
and my teacher will ask me why.

I could say I was riding a furry floo
and baking a mashoo pie.

I could tell her that 40 nolly baboons
came dada-lumfing by.

I could tell her I met some ugly meez
and a greelus talking fly.

I guess I'll tell her the plain old truth
or at least I guess I'll try.
I didn't get my homework done
'cause I forgot—that's why.

Yummy!

Writing a Made-Up-Words Poem

Activate Prior Knowledge

Invite children to recall words they or younger family members may have made up when learning to talk—words they used in place of those they were not yet able to pronounce. Children may enjoy remembering the primary words they used for a sibling's name or a well-loved stuffed animal. Explain that although these words (and the words younger siblings or cousins may have used) sound funny to others, they were useful because they truly had meaning. The person who said them knew what he or she meant, even if others had to decode the meaning or found the words funny.

Share the Poem

1. Distribute copies of the poem (page 85), write it on chart paper, or copy it onto an overhead transparency.

2. Explain that today's poem is filled with made-up words, but that the poet intentionally wrote them that way.

3. Ask children to listen for the made-up words as you read the poem aloud. When you finish reading, have children point out the unfamiliar words and underline those that are made-up.

4. Ask children to tell what helped them identify the words that were made-up, which in most cases is because the word is quite silly and children have never heard it before.

5. Discuss the poet's reasons for using these words. Explain that this type of poem is called a made-up-words poem because the poet used words she invented just to make the poem fun and silly.

Scaffold Using the Graphic Organizer

1. Tell children that the class will plan and write a made-up-words poem. Together, choose a topic that would offer many opportunities to name objects, such as "Why I Didn't Go to Bed on Time" or "Why I Didn't Clean My Room Today."

2. Photocopy and distribute the graphic organizer (page 88). If possible, copy the organizer onto an overhead transparency or enlarge it so that you can model how to use it.

3. Write the title of your poem at the top of the graphic organizer. Then complete the first sentence frame, repeating what didn't happen or get done (go to bed on time, didn't clean up) and who will be asking for a reason (perhaps a parent or other caregiver).

4. Ask children to brainstorm a list of excuses someone might give (for why a child didn't go to bed on time or why a child didn't clean his or her room, for example). Encourage children to think of ridiculous reasons. Make them wild and fun! Write these on the organizer.

5. As a class, choose one or two words to circle in each excuse. Then replace these with words that you and children make up. Write each made-up word above each circled word.

6. Number the excuses in the order children would like to mention them in the poem. Then write the poem on a sheet of chart paper, inserting the made-up words. End the poem with the author's last lines, again filling in what the narrator of the poem didn't do.

7. Read the poem aloud, asking children to listen carefully and to check that the poem makes sense with its made-up words in place.

8. On the same day or during another session, revisit your made-up-words poem and remind children of the steps they took to create it. Then give them a fresh copy of the organizer. Following the same techniques used above, help children use the organizer to plan their own made-up-words poems. When you feel children are ready, have them copy their poems onto a separate sheet of paper.

Name _____ Date _____

Plan Your Made-Up-Words Poem

1. The title of my poem is "Why I Didn't _____"

2. Fill in the blanks: I didn't _____
and my _____ will ask me why.

3. Write your excuses on the lines below.

I could _____

I could _____

I could _____

4. Circle one or two words in each excuse.
5. Write a made-up word above each word you circle.
6. Number your excuses in the order you want to use them.
7. End your poem with the four lines below.

I guess I'll tell the plain old truth
or at least I guess I'll try.

I didn't _____
'cause I forgot—that's why.

Big Box of Excuses

Name _____ Date _____

Plan Your Made-Up-Words Poem

1. The title of my poem is "Why I Didn't _____."

2. Fill in the blanks: I didn't _____,

and my _____ will ask me why.

3. Write your excuses on the lines below.

I could _____

_____.

I could _____

_____.

I could _____

_____.

4. Circle one or two words in each excuse.

5. Write a made-up word above each word you circle.

6. Number your excuses in the order you want to use them.

7. End your poem with the four lines below.

I guess I'll tell the plain old truth

or at least I guess I'll try.

I didn't _____,

'cause I forgot—that's why.

Big
Box
of
Excuses

What Is White?

A dream feels white.
The waves sound white.
The morning fog smells white.

A tear tastes white.
The clouds look white.
And so does laughing
and candlelight.

The snow sounds white
on winter nights.
In the morning light,
the whole world
          tastes
                and smells
                    and looks
                        and feels
                            and sounds
                                like the color white
                                    is all around.

89

Writing a Mixed-Up-Senses Poem

Activate Prior Knowledge

Begin by helping children review the five senses: *seeing, hearing, smelling, touching,* and *tasting*. Write each sense on chart paper as children name it. (See Writing a Senses Poem, page 58, for more.)

Then talk with children about what it means when something is mixed-up. For example, wearing boots on your hands and gloves on your feet is mixed up! Invite children to go to a silly place inside their thoughts and think of other events they could mix up for fun, such as ice skating in the ocean and reading books backwards and upside down.

Share the Poem

1. Review with children what it means when something is mixed up. Then tell them that in today's poem, the five senses are mixed up! The poet used her imagination to write so that things they can see but not hear now make sounds. Things they can hear but not see now have color.

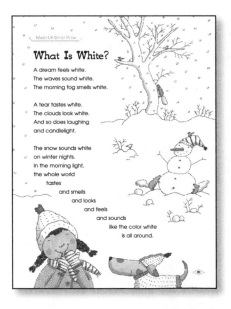

2. Distribute copies of the poem (page 89), write it on chart paper, or copy it onto an overhead transparency.

3. Read the poem aloud, and then invite children to read along with you.

4. Ask children to find places in the poem where the poet mixed up the senses (*a dream feels white; the waves sound white,* and so on). Underline each mixed-up reference.

5. Talk about the mix-ups. Ask: "Why is it mixed up to say that ocean waves sound white? How can a person's laugh be white?" Help children understand that white is a color and that people usually see it rather than smell, taste, touch, or hear it. Yet in this poem, the poet says "The waves sound white." She is mixing up the senses to surprise the reader.

6. Ask children to find the line in the poem that shows the sense of sight in the way we normally use it: *The clouds look white.* Invite them to suppose why the poet chose to put one line that is not mixed up among the many that are.

Scaffold Using the Graphic Organizer

1. Tell children that the class will plan and write a mixed-up senses poem. Together, choose a color other than white.

2. Photocopy and distribute the graphic organizer (page 92). If possible, copy the organizer onto an overhead transparency or enlarge it so that you can model how to use it.

3. Using the color you have chosen, write the title of your poem on the organizer, such as "What Is Green?"

4. Encourage children to talk and think about the senses as they relate to the color you've chosen. Ask them to suggest what looks, sounds, smells, feels, and tastes like it. Write each suggestion on the corresponding can of paint.

5. On chart paper or an overhead, help children compose a sentence using each word. Have children number the sentences in the order they want to use them in their poem. Then copy the sentences, in order, onto a fresh sheet of paper or on an overhead. Help children write a poem using the ideas you have listed on the organizer.

6. On the same day or during another session, revisit your mixed-up senses poem and remind children of the steps they took to create it. Then give them a fresh copy of the organizer. Following the same techniques used above, help children use the organizer to plan their own mixed-up senses poems. When you feel children are ready, have them write their poems on a separate sheet of paper.

Name _____

Date _____

Plan Your Mixed-Up-Senses Poem

1. Write a title that tells your color. "What is _____ ?"

2. Use your imagination to answer these questions. Write in the cans of paint.

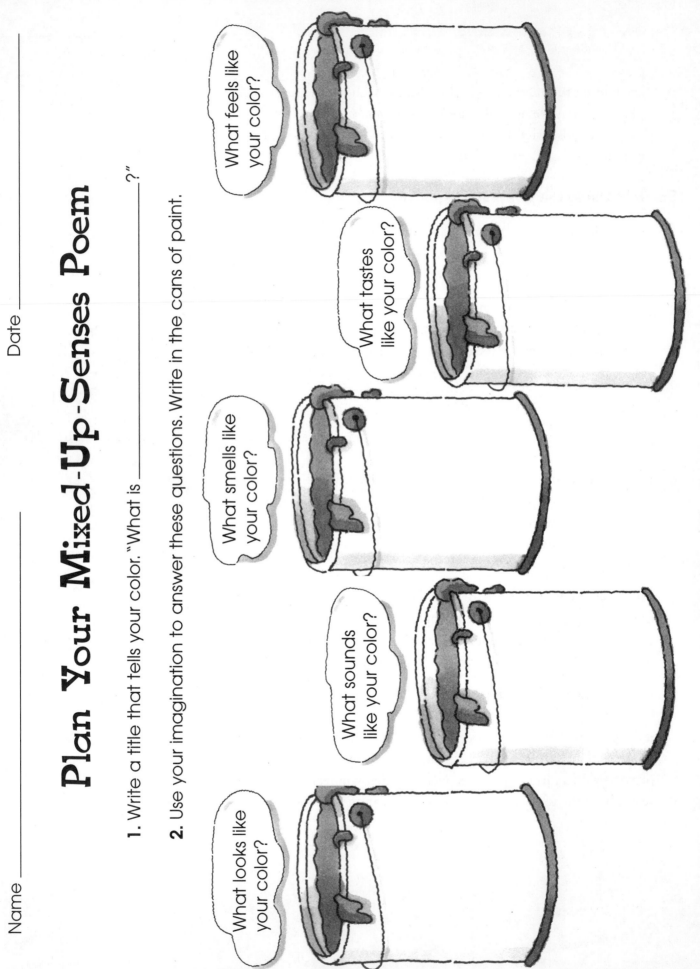

What feels like your color?

What tastes like your color?

What smells like your color?

What sounds like your color?

What looks like your color?

Hey, Daddy Longlegs

Hey, daddy longlegs,
where are you?

**I'm living right behind
the glue.**

I'll find your web,
and wipe it away.

**I'll spin another web
today.**

Let's make a deal.
Come on, okay?

**Sounds good to me.
Whatever you say.**

I won't destroy
the spinning you do.

**And . . .
I'll stay out of sight
so I don't startle you.**

Writing a Conversation Poem

Activate Prior Knowledge

Discuss the word *conversation*. Ask children to name other words for "conversation," such as *talk*, *chat*, *gabfest*, *discussion*. Guide them to understand that a conversation is oral dialogue between two or more people, in which they share ideas and opinions. Invite them to name times when people have conversations—such as when they are making plans, working out a problem, or asking for advice.

Share the Poem

1. Distribute copies of the poem (page 93), write it on chart paper, or copy it onto an overhead transparency.

2. Tell children that today's poem is called a *conversation poem*. Explain that there are two different speakers in the poem: a child and a daddy longlegs spider. (Point out that the spider's words appear darker than the child's. This is to help the reader realize that the characters take turns talking.)

3. Read the poem aloud. Then divide the class into two groups. Help each group read one part of the poem, as the child or the spider.

Scaffold Using the Graphic Organizer

1. Tell children that the class will plan and write a conversation poem. Together, choose two characters for the conversation. Select characters who might have a lot to say to one another, prompting exciting dialogue. Examples include a cat and mouse and a human and mosquito.

2. Photocopy and distribute the graphic organizer (page 96). If possible, copy the organizer onto an overhead transparency or enlarge it so that you can model how to use it.

3. Write the names of both characters at the top of the organizer.

4. Help students generate conversation that might take place between the two characters. For example, a cat might say to a mouse, "Come out, little mouse! You don't fool me!" The mouse might respond, "I'm here in my mouse hole, but you cannot see!"

5. Encourage children to think through several lines of dialogue before you write it. Encourage them to plan how the conversation might end so that it does not drag on without a purpose.

6. Write the dialogue in the appropriate conversation bubbles on the organizer. Then rewrite the poem on chart paper, deleting the line numbers.

7. On the same day or during another session, revisit your conversation poem and remind children of the steps they took to create it. Then give them a fresh copy of the organizer. Following the same techniques used above, help children use the organizer to plan their own conversation poems. When you feel children are ready, have them copy their poems onto a separate sheet of paper.

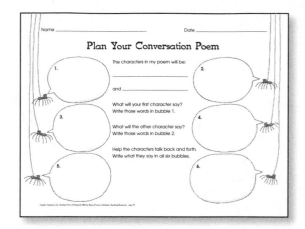

POETRY TIP

Children may wish to work in pairs the first time they write a conversation poem. In that case, one child will write in conversation bubbles 1, 3, and 5 while the other responds by writing in bubbles 2, 4, and 6.

Name _____

Date _____

Plan Your Conversation Poem

The characters in my poem will be:

_____

and _____

What will your first character say?
Write those words in bubble 1.

What will the other character say?
Write those words in bubble 2.

Help the characters talk back and forth.
Write what they say in all six bubbles.

1.

2.

3.

4.

5.

6.

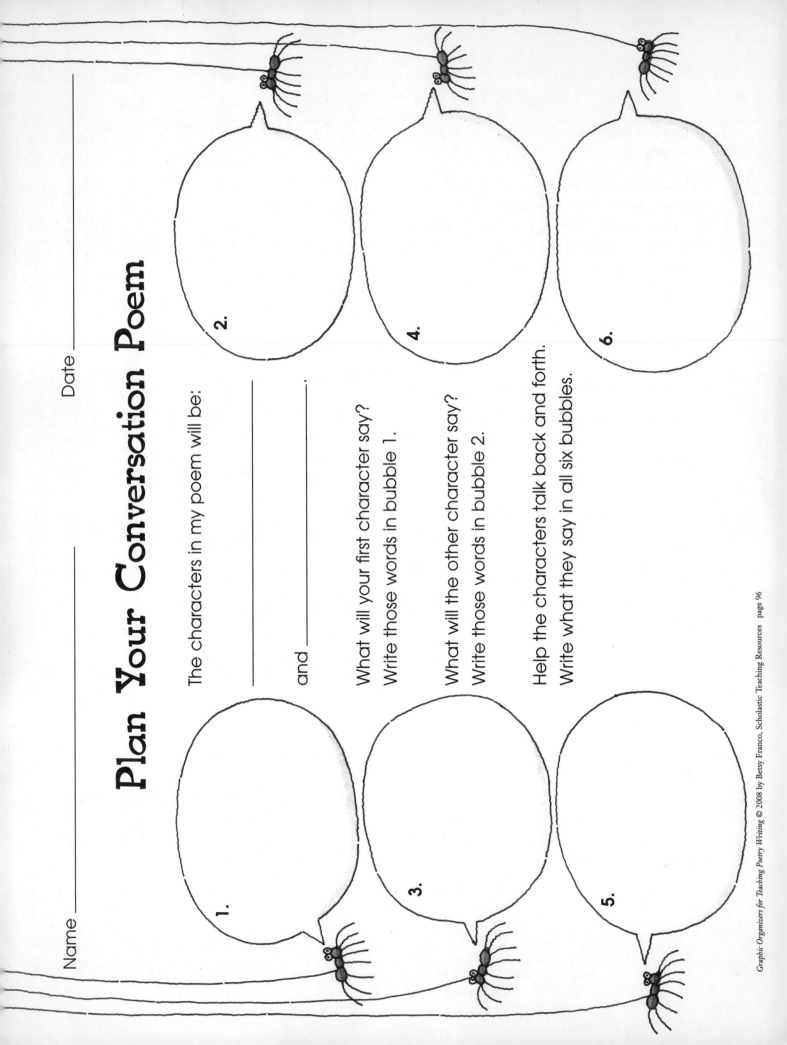